Kerry Kern

Siberian Huskies

Everything about Purchase, Care, Nutrition, Behavior, and Training

Filled with Full-color Photographs
Illustrations by Michele Earle-Bridges

D1510231

BARRON'S

2 CONTENTS

HISTORY OF SIBERIAN HUSKIES

The Chukchi Dog

For more than 1,000 years a tribe of people known as the Chukchi have inhabited the Arctic coastal region of northern Siberia—a land where the extremes of winter make life a daily challenge just for survival. It is there that the Chukchi dog, the progenitor of today's Siberian Husky, was developed.

Over many generations of breeding, the Chukchi developed the breed of dog that most suited their needs. Although their permanent home was inland, the Chukchi hunters worked primarily along the coast, with seal as their main food source. The hunters' catch was not so heavy as to require large dogs capable of pulling great weight. Instead, the Chukchi hunters needed a dog that could withstand extended exposure to the low temperatures, that could pull a light-to-moderate load quickly over long distances, and that could expend a minimum amount of energy in the process. The less energy the dog used on its work, the more it had left to protect it from the weather.

Quick, small working dogs that were docile and intelligent enough to work in teams proved most suited to the work and terrain. They had to be hard, eager workers that had enough common sense and dedication to their task to keep from constantly tangling them-

Siberian Huskies have been trained as sled dogs for many years.

selves in the lines of the sled. The Chukchi so valued their dogs that they often took them into their homes as guardians for their possessions and as companions for their children. This, no doubt, accounts for much of the gentleness in the Siberian Husky personality.

The Chukchi dog's most important trait was its instinct and desire to run, seemingly endlessly. Because of its moderate size, it was able to run far and fast, but it could not pull much weight. Therefore, teams of up to 20 dogs at a time were required to pull the hunters' loads. The Chukchi were able to breed a dog that combined all these traits, and today's Siberian Husky traces to those dogs.

The fate of the Chukchi dog—and the birth of the Siberian Husky breed—are tied to several historical events, primarily in Russia. In the eighteenth century, Russian cossacks began a march across Siberia to conquer the land and to attain all of its resources, primarily fur. Most people living in this northern area were primitive tribal groups who were unable to compete with the advanced weaponry of the invading Russian army. The Chukchi people were able to withstand conquest, however, because their sled dogs always kept them ahead of the advancing military forces. Although they could not fight, they could run—efficiently. The Chukchi were accustomed to the Siberian weather; the Russian soldiers were not, and they suffered great losses.

The Chukchi actually forced the cossacks to abandon their quest to conquer all of northern Siberia. The Chukchi lured the Russian forces into a mountain pass, in which all escape routes were blocked. Using only sharpened rocks and spears, the Chukchi inflicted substantial casualties on the Russians, who subsequently withdrew from the area.

The Chukchi people and their dogs existed peaceably in Siberia for many years after this conflict. By the close of the nineteenth century, the Chukchi dog had been discovered by Alaskan traders, imported into the Northwest Territory, and renamed the Siberian Husky. This importation proved very important for the survival of the breed.

In the early 1900s, the monarchy in Russia was overthrown and replaced by a Communist regime, vowing to do away with all "bourgeois" and elite aspects of Russian life. By the 1930s, the forces of Communism reached the Arctic North. Because Chukchi dogs were highly revered and desired by the Chukchi people, those members of the tribe who bred and maintained the finest dogs had assumed a leadership position and measure of wealth. Such people were viewed as hindrances to the forces of collectivization, and most were imprisoned or killed. In just a few years, the Chukchi dog breed all but disappeared from Siberia.

Dog Sledding Begins

Unlike the breed's fate in Russia, the Siberian Husky was taking hold in Alaska. Dog sledding had become not only a means of transportation, but also a popular sport for the adventurers who had journeyed north in search of gold. Local races quickly evolved into large events

with numerous entries. A lawyer named Albert Fink undertook the task of regulating the dogsled events and helped formalize the sport.

The dogs used in the early races were primarily Alaskan sled dogs, originally bred to haul freight. They were larger and stronger than Siberian Huskies, but were not as quick. They were, however, well adapted to the terrain and had great competitive spirit. In 1908, William Goosak, a Russian fur trader, entered a team of Chukchi dogs in the All-Alaska sled race from Nome. Although Goosak hired a local driver familiar with the 408-mile course to lead the team, the driver was unfamiliar with the Chukchi dog style of dog sledding. The team finished third against the experienced dogs and drivers, but the dogs' speed and enthusiasm attracted a lot of attention to the breed. Many Chukchi dogs subsequently were imported from Siberia.

The first sled driver to gain notoriety on the sled dog circuit using Siberian Huskies was Leonhard Seppala, a Norwegian who had emigrated to Alaska early in the twentieth century. He inherited a well-trained team of Huskies that had originally been scheduled to drive explorer Roald Amundsen to the North Pole. When the expedition was canceled because of World War I, the dogs were given to Seppala. Over the next few years, Seppala's Siberian Husky teams beat all racers throughout the Northwest. His Huskies were all but unbeatable in the annual 25-mile Borden Cup Race in Nome.

In January 1925, Seppala and his Huskies earned a place in history. During that winter, an epidemic of diphtheria broke out in Nome, and local doctors did not have adequate supplies of the required diphtheria serum. At the time, Nome was connected to the lower territories only by telephone; the nearest railroad station was more than 650 miles south near Anchorage. Seppala was asked to go and collect the serum by dogsled—in a race against time. Seppala and his team headed south along the Tanana and Yukon Rivers and the Bering Sea—some of the most treacherous sections of Alaska's wilderness. A relay team of 15 sleds and dogs was sent north with the serum to meet Seppala, as the world waited. On the day Seppala met up with the relay team (after mushing nearly 170 miles) he had already traveled more than 40 miles in blizzard conditions; he retrieved the serum and immediately headed back to Nome, posting another 40 miles before resting briefly. His team of 20 dogs amassed nearly 350 miles in this journey. The teams from the south ran relays of approximately 50 miles each and contributed greatly to the success of this mission.

News reports of the feats of Seppala's dogs brought great acclaim to the breed. It created a demand for Siberian Huskies, especially by sledding enthusiasts in New England. Because Alaskan breeders were unable to fill the requests they received, many interested fanciers imported dogs directly from Siberia. These proved to be the last substantial imports before the breed disappeared in its homeland. Today's Husky that is bred specifically for sled work is a slightly stockier and smaller than the specimens seen in the show ring.

Modern Dogsled Races

Like the early Chukchi hunters, Alaskan breeders have worked hard to produce the breed of dog most suited to the northern climate and the requirements of modern dogsled racing. Breeders have used Alaskan Malamutes, Siberian Huskies, and other native dogs to produce a strain of sledding dogs now termed Alaskan Huskies. Today, Siberian Husky teams compete in many aspects of dogsled racing, but they have limited success against Alaskan Husky specialists in the traditional long-distance hauling races.

The Siberian Husky specializes in races involving speed, agility, and maneuverability. Common classes at dogsled races include those for three dogs running 3 miles, six dogs running 6 miles, eight dogs running 9 miles, and the unlimited class in which teams of up to 20 dogs race 14 or more miles.

Training a Siberian Husky dogsled team is a year-round process. During the months when snow is not available, the dogs must still be conditioned. During warmer weather, the teams are worked on training sleds that are on wheels for each movement. During this preparation, the dogs become accustomed to the harness and the weight they will need to pull, and, most importantly, they learn to work and run together as a team.

Today's most famous dogsled race, the annual Iditarod race from Anchorage to Nome, commemorates the historic journey of Leonhard Seppala and his Siberian Huskies. The course is more than 1,100 miles and currently offers a purse of $250,000, with $50,000 going to the winner. A record time of a little less than 11 days was posted in 1987 by three-time winner Susan Butcher and her Alaskan Huskies.

The "Triple Crown" of dogsled racing is the Iditarod, the more sedate Alpirod in Europe, and the 1,000-mile Yukon Quest from the Yukon Territory to Fairbanks.

Dogsled racing is monitored worldwide by the International Federation of Sleddog Sports, a coalition of sled dog racing associations and 18 member countries.

CONSIDERATIONS BEFORE BUYING

The Right Dog for You?

The decision to purchase a dog, especially a Siberian Husky, should be made only after you have evaluated the suitability of that breed to your home and daily life. The following questions may guide you in your evaluation.

Does owning a dog suit my lifestyle? A good owner must train the dog thoroughly in the basic commands and supply it with daily love, attention, adequate housing, and an outlet for its energy. The Siberian Husky is not a good breed for those who work long hours and leave their pets alone. To thrive, Siberians need companionship, ample space, and a good dose of exercise. Owners must make a lifelong commitment of personal attention and daily walks with the dog for approximately the next ten years.

Can I properly care for a Siberian Husky? A Husky can be quite expensive to maintain. Aside from the initial purchase price, which can range anywhere from $400 to more than $1,000, an owner must provide routine veterinary care and an ample, nutritious diet. Such costs are considerable and constant throughout the dog's life.

Is a puppy wanted by everyone in the household? Despite good intentions, owners sometimes find that other family members view the household pet—especially a puppy— as a nuisance. Because this usually spells disas-

These two Siberian Huskies are enjoying the snow.

ter for the dog, think carefully and discuss how owning a dog may affect the existing household routine and the members of the home before you commit to pet ownership. Similarly, an adult Husky—in its enthusiasm to jump and greet a visitor—can easily knock a child or an elderly person over, possibly into furniture or on to hard surfaces. You must consider the ability of all members of the household to live with the dog. Some breeders recommend that these dogs—while loving toward all—should not be placed in homes with children younger than three years old.

Do I really want a puppy? Puppies require a significant amount of attention, monitoring, and training. They will need frequent walks and access to the outside during the housebreaking process. There will be accidents, and there may be damage from chewing. An older dog may be more appropriate for those who cannot be home during the day.

Do I have the time to exercise a Siberian Husky? More than any other consideration, willingness to exercise the Siberian is of utmost importance for owners. Merely giving them access to a fenced yard is not enough. These dogs need at least one lengthy walk daily, with a workout of some kind along the way. Although Siberian Huskies are lovable and friendly, they should not be living with sedentary owners. A Siberian Husky should never ever be placed on an outside leash and left for long periods. If this is your plan for exercising your dog, choose another breed.

Purchasing Your Siberian

If you have answered "yes" to all the preceding questions, the search for your Husky can begin. Over the years, Siberian Husky breeders have worked steadfastly on protecting against careless overbreeding, which often happens after a breed becomes popular. Despite this breed's popularity, locating a large number of quality Husky puppies is not as easy as you would think. Most Husky owners and breeders do not produce a large number of litters. They are careful about which dogs are bred and where the puppies are placed.

Show Dog, Sled Dog, or Pet?

To find the best source for your dog, you must first decide what functions the dog will be expected to fulfill. Are you looking for a show competitor, a sled dog, or a companion? If you are looking for a potential winner in competitive contests, you need to do thorough research and make a careful selection.

Selecting a puppy destined to be a show dog is always a gamble. Most puppies are purchased at eight to ten weeks of age—a time of rapid development. What the dog will look like when mature cannot be accurately assessed at this time, only predicted. Selections made while a Siberian puppy is still growing (until approximately 12 to 15 months) are "best guesses" and should therefore be based on pedigree and the breeder's knowledge of how their dogs mature. Because a preliminary evaluation of breed type can be made more accurately at four to six months of age, hold off purchasing a show

prospect until then, if possible. "Show-quality" puppies will be expensive, so a careful selection is imperative.

If you want a sled dog, you should locate an established kennel that actively participates in the sport. Do not be surprised if they have little available stock, however, because these breeders generally will keep the puppies with best potential for themselves until they can more thoroughly evaluate the puppies for speed and desire at a later age. For novice sledding enthusiasts, most well-bred Huskies should fill the bill for desire and pulling ability.

People who want a pet Husky have many options. If there is a good Siberian kennel in your area, preferably one that produces show winners, ask if they have any pet-quality dogs available. These puppies or slightly older dogs will be well-bred, quality Siberians that have been eliminated from competitive status for some minor fault that makes them unsuitable for the show ring. With such dogs the pedigrees of both dam and sire are known, and the puppies have been raised during the formative stages by knowledgeable people. The price of such puppies usually will be from several hundred dollars and up.

Pet Quality

Pet-quality Siberian Huskies can also be bought from pet stores or neighborhood litters. If you are considering a pet-store dog, be sure to find out where the puppy was purchased and get as much information as possible on its initial care. Although quality pet stores will deal only with knowledgeable and reputable local breeders, there have been cases where unscrupulous shop owners have purchased dogs from "puppy mills" in the midwestern United States, where dogs are mass produced from whatever breeding stock is available. Quality should always be your primary concern, not easy availability. The price for a purebred dog from a pet shop will often be the same as pet-quality and sometimes show-quality dogs from private kennels.

Neighborhood litters are a common source of pet-quality dogs, and the purchase price generally is quite reasonable. You should ask to see both the mother and father's registration papers before you buy any puppy. Without this documentation, the puppy's litter will be ineligible for registration with the American Kennel Club (AKC). If the breeder cannot supply these papers, you cannot be sure you are buying a registerable purebred—and the purchase price you pay should reflect this. With random breedings such as this, the parents are likely to be from diverse genetic backgrounds. Although the resulting puppies will almost always be fine representatives of the breed, there is little chance that you are buying a future conformation champion.

A small number of Huskies find homes through the work of national rescue leagues, which stay in close contact with shelters and retrieve most purebred Siberian Huskies, should they turn up. They then try to find the original owners and, if necessary, place the dog in a suitable home. The names and addresses of local, regional, and national Siberian Husky organizations and their corresponding secretaries can be obtained by writing the AKC (see page 92 for the address). The AKC magazine, *Purebred Dogs: American Kennel Gazette,* is published monthly and contains a breed column, a list of advertising kennels, articles on all aspects of dog care, information on upcoming shows, and lists of recent winners.

Remember: not all breeders are working for the betterment of the breed. Be sure to check credentials, and stay clear of anyone who seems more interested in profit than the welfare of this breed.

Evaluating a Puppy

Regardless of how you intend to use your Siberian Husky, it should be carefully evaluated for general health and essential breed characteristics. Start your evaluation at the beginning, because the care a litter receives during the first few weeks of life can have lifelong effects. The living quarters must be clean, fairly spacious, and parasite-free. There should be signs that the owner has interacted with puppies during the early days, not just left them alone with the mother in some secluded spot.

Look not only at a puppy, but at its litter as a whole. Purchasing the puppy from a poor litter is a risky proposition. Ask the breeder why the parents were selected for breeding and whether they had been checked for a predisposition toward hip dysplasia.

The Parents

You usually can get a pretty good idea of a puppy's probable size and type by looking at both the dam (mother) and sire (father). Often only the dam is available, as the sire may be from another kennel. Don't be too critical by the dam's outward appearance, however. She has just endured the whelping and nursing of her litter, so she may appear thin or run down. The owner probably will have a prepregnancy picture that can give you a better indication. Acceptable behavior for the dam would be to act aloof, calm, and stable; she may be curious

Your puppy will need lots of training.

or friendly toward you, but she should not be penalized for being a bit reserved or standoffish. This is a breed trait. She should be responsive to her owner and should respond to assurances that all is well.

Try to get as much information as possible regarding the sire. Ask if this breeding pair have ever been mated previously. If yes, you may be able to see some of the maturing dogs from a previous litter or ask for the name and phone number of an owner of one of these dogs. This is especially important if you are purchasing a show prospect.

If you take the time to carefully check your puppy's background, it will make things much easier when you finally bring it home.

There are many important considerations to take into account when you are choosing a puppy.

Overall Appearance

When evaluating an eight-week-old puppy, first look at its overall appearance, bearing in mind that a growing puppy is likely to appear somewhat awkward and out of balance—different skeletal areas grow at different rates. It should be vigorous and plump (but not bloated, which can indicate a worm infestation). A thriving puppy is clean and pleasant smelling, its eyes are clear and not runny, and there is no discharge in the ears.

The Husky puppy should appear compact, with a deep chest and level back. It should move effortlessly and be quite active. Siberians are not timid and should respond cheerfully when engaged into play. A well-socialized puppy will not be intimidated by this, although it may be a little reserved. It should submit to gentle handling and allow you to physically inspect it. A slight variation in size among littermates and between the sexes is normal, and the largest puppy should not be deemed most desirable simply on this account. Important breed characteristics are the almond-shaped eyes and the "fox" tail. The "masks" that many Huskies have around the face are present from birth and may intensify with age.

What Age Is Best?

Although there is no set answer to the "best age" question, most breeders believe that puppies should be at least seven weeks old before being separated from their litter. At eight to twelve weeks of age, puppies are in a developmental stage known as the "human socialization period." This is the best time for a puppy to learn how to live happily with humans. A dog that remains with its litter and receives little contact with humans during this time will have its primary bond with dogs rather than humans.

It is also vital that the puppy is not removed much *before* eight weeks of age—during the canine socialization period. During the weeks spent with its pack, a dog learns how to get along with other animals. If removed too early, the poorly socialized dog may react aggressively or submissively when it meets other dogs. The end result can be fighters or "fear biters" who easily are upset and prone to unexpectedly lashing out at other dogs and people. Puppies produced in the "puppy mills" often suffer from improper socialization because they are removed too young from their litter to arrive at retail outlets by eight weeks of age.

The greatest advantage of purchasing a puppy (besides being able to play with it during its most adorable stage) is that the owner is able to influence the dog's interaction with its environment. A Siberian Husky should never be placed on an outside leash and left for long periods. If this is your plan for exercising your dog, choose another breed. If you select an older Siberian puppy, be sure it has been raised with lots of human contact and interaction rather than left solely with its litter. Such a dog will be able to adapt quickly to a new home with humans, whereas a dog that has always been surrounded by its pack will feel isolated by such a change.

The Purchase Agreement

Hopefully, selecting your Siberian puppy has been an enjoyable experience. You must now formalize the agreement by putting all the terms of the deal in writing. Be precise and list not only the purchase price, but also the terms of the guarantee and what documentation will be supplied.

To guarantee that the puppy is healthy, most breeders will allow new owners a certain number of days to have the puppy examined by their personal veterinarian. Get the specific terms of the deal in writing—a verbal promise will get you nowhere legally. The agreement should specify whether a sick dog will be replaced with a healthy puppy or if the purchaser's money will be returned.

When dealing with a kennel or pet shop, the new owner of a purebred Siberian Husky should receive the puppy's AKC registration application at the time of the purchase. The application should include the names and AKC numbers of the sire and dam, information on the litter from which the puppy was whelped, and the name and address of the person to whom ownership is being transferred. The new owner must list two possible names for the puppy and complete all missing information. Processing the paperwork should take about three to four weeks, if all is in order.

Established breeders most likely will have registered the puppy's litter with the AKC shortly after birth and should have received these applications prior to the sale of any of the puppies. If the application is unavailable, the new owner must get a signed bill of sale from the breeder that lists the breed, sex, and color of the puppy; its date of birth; and the registered names (with numbers) of the sire and dam. Without this information, the AKC likely will be unable to register the dog.

Kennels that breed Huskies strictly for show purposes may have some additional purchase terms. The breeder may want to be involved with the future breeding of the dog or may stipulate that it will be sold only on the condition that it is shown in competition for its championship. Such concerned kennels may agree to sell a pet-quality dog only on the condition that it not be bred and may even withhold registration papers until proof is supplied that the dog has been neutered. In exchange for such terms, the breeder often will offer an attractive selling price for the dog.

UNDERSTANDING SIBERIAN HUSKIES

Pack Behavior

Many theories state that the first doglike animals on earth date to around 600,000 B.C. Domesticated dogs date back nearly 20,000 years, with their closest recognizable ancestor being the wolf. During this time, life was extremely harsh, and food supplies were limited. These primitive animals learned the benefits of grouping together for survival. A pack behavior evolved, entailing various levels of hierarchy patterns among the dogs. The most assertive dog assumed the leadership position, leaving the other pack members to fall in line behind.

This pack behavior taught dogs the value of social cooperation and helped the progenitors of today's domestic dog and early man to form their first alliance—presumably as a result of a mutual need to hunt together for food. As time passed, man learned how to breed dogs selectively to attain certain goals: fast runners, good hunters, avid watchdogs. Such useful qualities served humans well. Over time, a bond of friendship also arose, and the first dual-purpose dogs developed: workers and companions.

Behavior Patterns

Modern dogs have inherited many of the traits utilized by the earliest members of their

Siberian Huskies are gentle, well-mannered dogs.

species, though rarely are they called on to utilize these long-hidden survival instincts. Although pack behavior still exists, dogs have had to learn to adapt to the rules of the human pack. Domestication has tempered the aggressiveness that early dogs needed for survival, but through selective breeding many of the characteristics and traits that man found most useful survived.

Siberian Huskies originated in a land with some of the harshest weather on earth to serve their owners as sled dogs and companions. In other terrains, dogs of various structures and temperaments evolved to serve the particular needs of their owners. Even though many distinct breeds exist, all dogs share a common heritage and a basic means of expression, which is exhibited in their communication methods.

Hierarchy

If left to their own accord, when grouped together, unfamiliar dogs will instinctively begin to establish a hierarchy for this new pack. The most dominant dogs immediately will vie for top position. They will stand well up on their feet, snarl, and try to intimidate any perceived opponent. An inspection of the anal area generally is in order for each of the dogs. Fierce growling can ensue, and occasionally a fight may break out, but this usually is short-lived, as one animal will recognize its vulnerability and yield to the more dominant dog. The emerging leader often is referred to as the "alpha" dog.

Such maneuvering for power also will occur between dog and owner, although more often this is a war of wits rather than a physical confrontation. If the human does not exhibit what the dog perceives to be proper leadership qualities, the dog will think it is entitled to rule its pack and will try to do so. Owners must be aware of this and exhibit an assertive, consistent manner when dealing with the dog—especially when willful disobedience occurs. The dog must understand that it is subordinate to *all* humans in its pack, not only one primary master, and this instruction should begin as soon as the puppy is introduced into the household. It already has been indoctrinated by its mother, the original alpha (that is, top dog), so it should learn quickly to accept its assigned place as pet—not leader—of the home.

Siberian Huskies are gentle dogs and not prone to viciousness. In a multidog household, however, some dogs instinctively may challenge the presence of other animals they believe are vying for the superior position in that pack. Acting up may also result from a mild case of jealousy, especially if an owner seems to favor one dog over others. On the whole, however, the Husky is so well mannered and amiable that all should get along peaceably.

Communication

Communication methods, such as vocalization, facial expression, and body language, basically are uniform among all breeds of dogs. Humans can learn to interpret more accurately the meaning of a dog's actions by being alert to what the dog's body language is showing (and also to what your body language and vocal tones are telling the dog). Your dog has a limited frame of reference. It must rely on the signals you give with your commands, vocal tones, and physical demeanor. Owners should pay attention to the differences among the various sounds the dog makes and the significance of the accompanying movements.

Body Language

A Siberian at ease will have a relaxed posture: its head and ears are up and its tail is at rest or moving slowly. When happy, the tail usually moves on a horizontal plane, the ears are up, and the dog may whine or give off some short barks. A dog inviting play often will drop its front to the ground while keeping its hindquarters up (and its tail will be wagging). When at attention, the dog's ears point more forward, the tail is more horizontal, and the dog appears more up on its toes.

An aggressive dog will have an angry expression, with its ears pointed directly forward or pulled against the side of the head, and it may bare its teeth and emit low growls. A fearful dog is perhaps the most dangerous. It does not look as menacing as the aggressive dog, but it is very unpredictable. The face is slightly tensed, and the ears are pulled against the head; the overall body position is lowered. If the dog feels threatened, it can lash out quickly from this position.

A submissive dog often is thought mistakenly to be a dog that is feeling "guilty." It assumes a lowered position, tail down and tucked under its belly, ears pointing back. It will avoid eye contact, and its eyes will look rolled down and whiter than usual. This dog is not feeling guilty (which is a human condition), but rather it is responding submissively to an authority more dominant than itself. In addition, a submissive dog may attempt to lick the mouth or hands of the dominant individual and then roll onto its back or even urinate as further indication of its submission.

Mood Indicators

A confused, upset dog may also assume a lowered stance, but it will not grovel or try to lick. Instead, it may pant rapidly, which is indicative of stress.

Facial expressions often can help an owner understand a dog's intent. Siberians are masters of "cute." They can look so sweet and innocent that it is hard to resist their charm.

The position and movement of the tail usually are good mood indicators. A Husky often carries its tail curled up and over its back rather than in the horizontal position that generally indicates contentment for other breeds. This position also can indicate excitement or heightened attention. A low-slung tail position indicates fear or apprehension.

The Owner's Role

Pay attention to the body language signals that your dog is giving you. Assess the situation and respond properly. These are the actions of a leader in the dog's view.

A dog will respond to its owner primarily by how it interprets that person's vocal tone and body language. This response, and the few basic command words it has been taught, are all it has to work with. The owner must, in turn, show the dog what is expected of it by example.

Positive Reinforcement

Dogs learn to obey by positive experiences; they learn to fear by negative ones. The follow-ing scenario is a classic example of miscommunication: after discovering a housebreaking "mistake" on the carpet, the owner yells, chastises, or even hits the dog, which is now crouched low to the floor in search of a safe place to hide. The owner interprets the dog's actions to be signs that it knows it has done wrong and is showing its guilt. In truth, the dog is submitting to the master in an act of self-preservation. It hears loud, angry tones, sees an angry expression, and reacts with fear. It has not been given any reason to associate its actions with the master's reactions. Nothing has been resolved here. The dog is afraid and confused; the owner has done nothing toward eliminating any similar mistakes.

The best way to encourage a dog to learn and retain information is through positive reinforcement. To be an effective leader you must show the dog what it is expected to do, and praise it highly when the task is accomplished. If mistakes are made, the dog should be corrected promptly and again shown the proper action. When the action finally is completed, the dog should then be praised.

Many factors complicate this learning process. Some Siberian Huskies are more intelligent than others, making them more capable learners. Many Huskies are stubborn or easily bored by training procedures, making them less willing learners. Some owners are better trainers than others. Although differences abound, both dog and owner can establish a system that works for them if they are willing to commit to the process.

If you encounter problems, try to evaluate what the cause may be: Is the dog confused? Is it testing my authority? Am I making my commands clear? Can the dog do what I am asking

of it? The answers to these questions will provide important clues to how well your dog understands your training program and how you may need to alter your methods to achieve the best results.

Digging

Siberian Huskies love to dig, especially down through layers of snow. They often dig a body-size hole—their "nest"—and lie down contentedly in it. They also will dig into the ground, which is an annoyance. The resulting muddy paws and destroyed flower beds can irritate even the most mellow owner, so be aware and prepare. Don't plant flowers in the dog's exercise area, and don't let the dog roam the flower garden without supervision. Check the

A dog's body language signals are important communication indicators.

dog's feet for dirt when it enters the house. You've got to work out a balance, as the dog will dig and take great pleasure in it.

All fencing in the yard should be buried to a depth that exceeds the digging capability of the dog, or the fence can be mounted in a solid foundation. Some Siberians also display a curious habit of giving a quick dig and then circling in the immediate area they are about to lie down in. (When this is your hardwood floor or carpeting, there is a problem.) This action is a throwback to the primitive times when dogs needed to carve out a nest for sleeping to protect themselves from the elements. Again, take your dog's habits and instincts into consideration when deciding where the dog is allowed to roam and sleep.

Living with a Siberian

A Siberian Husky's good points heavily outweigh its minor peculiarities. No dog is more loving and beguiling than a Siberian. It has a great zest for life, has boundless love in its heart, and a mischievous spirit. It is beautiful,

Speed and endurance are the traits for which the Siberian Husky is built.

with friendly eyes. Although not prone to much barking, it will let off a characteristic howl when making itself heard.

Don't count on the Siberian to be an ardent watchdog. It likes people, even strangers, too much to take offense at intruders. Although it can be relied on to bark when it hears someone outside, this is more a welcoming yowl than a warning growl.

The Siberian has an independent streak that often surfaces during training. When disinterested, a Siberian will not feign excitement to please its owners. A wise owner must work

around this by being a little more inventive than just following the textbook rules for training. When running is part of the routine, the Siberian is sure to perk up. Siberians love tag games and teasing. Use these games as other trainers would use tidbits to reward good work and more than likely you will keep the dog interested and learning—happily.

Companionship is vital in a Siberian's life. It will not do well alone. If it cannot have plenty of human attention, it must at least share its home with another dog to help it fill the hours until the owner returns. If left alone, it probably will become irrationally nervous and shy—traits foreign to the well-adjusted Husky. It also wants lots of exercise and time outdoors.

For safety, always remember that the Siberian will wander. It does not try actively to break away from its master; it just becomes enticed by any new sound or sight and will take off quickly after it. A Siberian can run very fast, and it is weak at sensing dangerous situations, such as approaching cars, open manholes, or deep trenches. Always keep the dog on a leash when outdoors and let it loose only in well-fenced areas. Without fail, if you leave a gate open, your Husky will go exploring.

The Quality Siberian

The Siberian Husky descends from what is called the spitz group—the dogs of the extreme northern climate that typically had thick, shaggy coats, pointed muzzles, plumy tails, and an incredible ability to work hard under the most extreme conditions. The other breeds in this group include the Alaskan Malamute, Samoyed, Keeshond, and Finnish Spitz.

The Siberian is most often compared with the Alaskan Malamute. Although the Malamute has similar markings, it is a larger dog of heavier bone that excels at pulling heavy loads over long distances. The Siberian is built for speed and endurance. It has a moderately compact body, with a deep chest and very muscular loins. It weighs only up to 60 pounds (132 kg) and has great pulling strength for its size. It is, in fact, one of the smallest of the working breeds.

The Siberian exhibits a wide range of coat colors, including occasionally an all-white. Most have a striking mask on the face. Its eyes may be either blue or brown, which makes it one of few breeds that have blue eyes as a desirable trait. Many Siberians have one blue and one brown eye, and this is perfectly acceptable and not to be penalized in the show dog.

Following is the official breed standard for the Siberian Husky, as devised by the national breed club and accepted by the AKC. It defines the ideal Siberian Husky. Although few dogs could measure up point by point with all requirements of the standard, it is the guide by which dogs are judged and serves as the goal for dedicated breeders.

Siberian Husky Standard

As approved by the American Kennel Club, October 8, 1990, effective November 28, 1990.

General Appearance

The Siberian Husky is a medium-sized working dog, quick and light on his feet and free and graceful in action. His moderately compact and well-furred body, erect ears and brush tail suggest his Northern heritage. His characteristic gait is smooth and seemingly effortless. He performs his original function in harness most

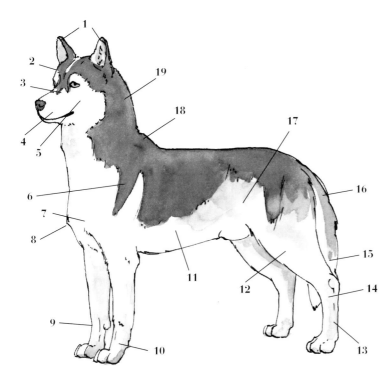

The anatomy of a
Siberian Husky:
1. ears
2. skull
3. stop
4. muzzle
5. cheek
6. shoulder
7. brisket
8. chest
9. forequarters
10. front pastern
11. rib cage
12. stifle
13. rear pastern
14. hock
15. hindquarters
16. tail
17. loin
18. withers
19. neckline

capably, carrying a light load at a moderate speed over great distances. His body proportions and form reflect this basic balance of power, speed, and endurance. The males of the Siberian Husky breed are masculine but never coarse; the bitches are feminine but without weakness of structure. In proper condition, with muscle firm and well developed, the Siberian Husky does not carry excess weight.

Size, Proportion, Substance

Height: Dogs, 21 to 23½ inches (53.3–59.7 cm) at the withers. Bitches, 20 to 22 inches (50.8–55.9 cm) at the withers.

Weight: Dogs, 45 to 60 pounds (20.4–27.2 kg). Bitches, 35 to 50 pounds (15.9–22.7 kg). Weight is in proportion to height. The measurements mentioned above represent the extreme height and weight limits with no preference given to either extreme. Any appearance of excessive bone or weight should be penalized. In profile, the length of the body from the point of the shoulder to the rear point of the croup is slightly longer than the height of the body from the ground to the top of the withers.

Disqualification: Dogs over 23½ inches and bitches over 22 inches.

The skeleton of a Siberian Husky.

Stop: The stop is well-defined and the bridge of the nose is straight from the stop to the tip. *Fault:* Insufficient stop.

Muzzle: Of medium length; that is, the distance from the tip of the nose to the stop is equal to the distance from the stop to the occiput. The muzzle is of medium width, tapering gradually to the nose, with the tip neither pointed nor square. *Faults:* Muzzle either too snipy or too coarse; muzzle too short or too long.

Nose: Black in gray, tan, or black dogs; liver in copper dogs; may be flesh-colored in pure white dogs. The pink-streaked "snow nose" is acceptable.

Lips: Are well pigmented and close fitting.

Teeth: Closing in a scissors bite. *Fault:* Any bite other than scissors.

Head

Expression: Is keen, but friendly; interested and even mischievous.

Eyes: Almond shaped, moderately spaced and set a trifle obliquely. Eyes may be brown or blue in color; one of each or parti-colored are acceptable. *Faults:* Eyes set too obliquely; set too close together.

Ears: Of medium size, triangular in shape, close fitting and set high on the head. They are thick, well furred, slightly arched at the back, and strongly erect, with slightly rounded tips pointing straight up. *Faults:* Ears too large in proportion to the head; too wide-set; not strongly erect.

Skull: Of medium size and in proportion to the body; slightly rounded on top and tapering from the widest point to the eyes. *Faults:* Head clumsy or heavy; head too finely chiseled.

The musculature of a Siberian Husky.

The Siberian Husky's coat does not hide the clean-cut outline of its body.

Neck, Topline, Body

Neck: Medium in length, arched and carried proudly erect when dog is standing. When moving at a trot, the neck is extended so that the head is carried slightly forward. *Faults:* Neck too short and thick; neck too long.

Chest: Deep and strong, but not too broad, with the deepest point being just behind and level with the elbows. The ribs are well-sprung from the spine but flattened on the sides to allow for freedom of action. *Faults:* Chest too broad; "barrel ribs;" ribs too flat or weak.

Back: The back is straight and strong, with a level topline from withers to croup. It is of medium length, neither cobby nor slack from excessive length. The loin is taut and lean, narrower than the rib cage, and with a slight tuck-up. The croup slopes away from the spine at an angle, but never so steeply as to restrict the rearward thrust of the hind legs. *Faults:* Weak or slack back; roached back; sloping topline.

Tail

The well-furred tail of fox-brush shape is set on just below the level of the topline, and is usually carried over the back in a graceful sickle curve when the dog is at attention. When carried up, the tail does not curl to either side of the body, nor does it snap flat against the back. A trailing tail is normal for the dog when in repose. Hair on the tail is of medium length and approximately the same length on top, sides, and bottom, giving the appearance of a round brush. *Faults:* A snapped or tightly curled tail; highly plumed tail; tail set too low or too high.

Forequarters

Shoulders: The shoulder blade is well laid back. The upper arm angles slightly backward from point of shoulder to elbow, and is never perpendicular to the ground. The muscles and ligaments holding the shoulder to the rib cage are firm and well-developed. *Faults:* Straight shoulders; loose shoulders.

Forelegs: When standing and viewed from the front, the legs are moderately spaced, parallel and straight, with the elbows close to the body and turned neither in nor out. Viewed from the side, pasterns are slightly slanted, with the pastern joint strong, but flexible. Bone is substantial but never heavy. Length of the leg from elbow to ground is slightly more than the distance from the elbow to the top of withers. Dewclaws on forelegs may be removed. *Faults:* Weak pasterns; too heavy bone; too narrow or too wide in the front; out at the elbows.

Feet: Oval in shape but not long. The paws are medium in size, compact and well-furred between the toes and pads. The pads are tough and thickly cushioned. The paws neither turn in nor out when the dog is in natural stance. *Faults:* Soft or splayed toes; paws too large and clumsy; paws too small and delicate; toeing in or out.

Hindquarters

When standing and viewed from the rear, the hind legs are moderately spaced and parallel. The upper thighs are well-muscled and powerful, the stifles well bent, the hock joint well defined and set low to the ground. Dewclaws, if any, are to be removed. *Faults:* Straight stifles, cowhocks, too narrow or too wide in the rear.

Coat

The coat of the Siberian Husky is double and medium in length, giving a well-furred appearance, but is never so long as to obscure the clean-cut outline of the dog. The undercoat is soft and dense and of sufficient length to support the outer coat. The guard hairs of the outer coat are straight and somewhat smooth-lying, never harsh nor standing straight off from the body. It should be noted that the absence of the undercoat during the shedding season is normal. Trimming of whiskers and fur between the toes and around the feet to present a neater appearance is permissible. Trimming the fur on any other part of the dog is not to be condoned and should be severely penalized. *Faults:* Long, rough, or shaggy coat; texture too harsh or too silky; trimming of the coat, except as permitted above.

Color

All colors from black to pure white are allowed. A variety of markings on the head is common, including many striking patterns not found in other breeds.

Gait

The Siberian Husky's characteristic gait is smooth and seemingly effortless. He is quick and light on his feet, and when in the show ring should be gaited on a loose lead at a moderately fast trot, exhibiting good reach in the forequarters and good drive in the hindquarters. When viewed from the front to rear while moving at a walk the Siberian Husky does not single-track, but as the speed increases the legs gradually angle inward until the pads are falling on a line directly under the longitudinal center of the body. As the pad marks converge, the forelegs and hind legs are carried straight forward, with neither elbows nor stifles turned in or out. Each hind leg moves in the path of the foreleg on the same side. While the dog is gaiting, the topline remains firm and level. *Faults:* Short, prancing or choppy gait, lumbering or rolling gait; crossing or crabbing.

Temperament

The characteristic temperament of the Siberian Husky is friendly and gentle, but also alert and outgoing. He does not display the posses-sive qualities of the guard dog, nor is he overly suspicious of strangers or aggressive with other dogs. Some measure of reserve and dignity may be expected in the mature dog. His intelligence, tractability, and eager disposition make him an agreeable companion and willing worker.

Summary

The most important breed characteristics of the Siberian Husky are medium size, moderate bone, well-balanced proportions, ease and freedom of movement, proper coat, pleasing head and ears, correct tail, and good disposition. Any appearance of excessive bone or weight, constricted or clumsy gait, or long, rough coat should be penalized. The Siberian Husky never appears so heavy or coarse as to suggest a freighting animal; nor is he so light and fragile as to suggest a sprint-racing animal. In both sexes the Siberian Husky gives the appearance of being capable of great endurance. In addition to the faults already noted, the obvious structural faults common to all breeds are as undesirable in the Siberian Husky as in any other breed, even though they are not specifically mentioned herein.

Disqualification

Dogs over 23½ inches and bitches over 22 inches.

CARING FOR SIBERIAN HUSKIES

The Siberian Husky's recent popularity can be traced to numerous factors: its beauty, intelligence, ease of care, loving personality, hardiness, and workmanship. Huskies excel as companions, but can also be trained to do many types of work (although guard dog duty definitely is not compatible with their people-loving nature). Adaptability is the key to the Siberian Husky. They do well in urban and rural settings; no climate is too extreme. The top requirement for owners is to provide the dog with companionship—both human and canine—from its earliest days. This is the key to a good beginning, one which will let the puppy develop to its fullest potential.

Getting Settled

Even though Siberian Huskies have been used throughout the breed's history as workers, they have *always* been raised as companions as well. This tractable, personable nature helps Husky puppies make the transition from litter to new home with relative ease. Huskies are very people-oriented, and they adapt well to the "human pack."

Before you bring your new puppy home, there are a few basic supplies to purchase.

1. food and water bowl (heavy enough not to slide while the dog is eating or drinking);

Huskies love their human companions and adapt well.

2. a high-quality puppy food (preferably the brand it has already been eating);

3. a bed or crate;

4. a puppy-size collar and lead;

5. a grooming brush and comb; and

6. a few safe chew toys.

The house should be puppy-proofed in much the same way as you would for a toddler. Although it might seem silly, the best way to check for potential dangers is to get down and inspect each room from the puppy's level. Remove not only all items that can be chewed or swallowed, but also any heavy items that are stored low enough to fall on an inquisitive puppy. Exposed electric cords are obvious targets during teething. Open staircases are very hazardous and should be closed off to ensure that the puppy will not fall down the stairs.

During its first few days in the home, the puppy will get its first—and probably lasting—impression about its new territory and owners. These early days should be enjoyable for the puppy. The owner should pay careful attention to the dog's actions and movements at all times. All members of the household will have to adapt to the new arrival. Be mindful of the puppy's whereabouts, as one of the most common injuries to a puppy is from being stepped on while under foot. Allowing the puppy to play too exuberantly also is dangerous. Jumping from too great a height can result in broken legs, hips, or shoulders.

Discipline

Living strictly among humans probably is new for your puppy. It will have to learn from the start that although there will be lots of love and fun experiences, there also will be corrections and discipline. A Siberian Husky puppy can be so charming that the owner will overlook its misdeeds. Don't be fooled into thinking that a puppy cannot learn while young or that trying to get the puppy to obey at an early age will ruin its spirit. A puppy can understand that some actions displease the owner and must be stopped. The puppy's dam probably has made it perfectly clear to her pups that there are limits to acceptable behavior and when rules are broken there is a correction. The owner must step into this leadership position. Dominance over the dog should be established while young and should be rein-

forced daily. Some easy ways to exert control are to keep the dog guessing and responding to the owner's wishes. Move the dog's food bowl every once in a while and pick it up momentarily during an occasional meal. When you give it back, praise the dog for its patience. Put the dog on its back and rub its belly and feet thoroughly. This is fun and establishes control. Change its sleeping place, even if just for a night or two, to prevent the dog from developing territoriality. Little actions like these mean a lot in imprinting that humans are in control.

It is never too early to begin teaching your puppy what is acceptable and what is unacceptable. Much learning occurs during the first days and weeks. An owner can help shape the behavior of the adult dog to come through careful monitoring and positive correction.

The First Day

When making the arrangements for picking up the puppy from its breeder, try to choose a time when you have several days free to devote to welcoming the dog to its new home (such as the beginning of a weekend or during a vacation period). Morning is best, because that gives you the whole day to spend with the dog before it must be left alone for its first night away from its littermates and dam. The more time you spend with the puppy, the easier the transition. If you bring a young puppy home one day and leave it alone the next while you go off to work or school, the puppy

When lifting a puppy, be sure to support it properly. Place one hand under the puppy's rear end and the other around its rib cage.

may feel abandoned and subsequently have a difficult time adjusting to its new home.

Speak to the puppy in soft, low tones and treat it gently. An easy way to enhance bonding is to get down frequently on the floor with the puppy. By playing with the puppy on its level you will seem more like a friendly, rather than towering, figure. Even though Siberian puppies are pretty rough-and-tumble, rough play is not recommended during the first few days. The puppy needs lots of attention and praise to help it feel reassured, comforted, and encouraged during these trying times.

As soon as you get home with the puppy, show it where its food and water bowls are located, and take it to the elimination area—it's never too early to begin housebreaking! Show it its sleeping quarters. You can then let the dog roam about its new home and explore on its own (while you monitor from nearby). Until reliably housetrained, a puppy should be confined whenever it is not being supervised directly.

Because a puppy of seven to nine weeks of age should still be receiving four meals a day, it will soon need to be fed. It will be nervous, bewildered, and may even have a slightly upset stomach, so reduce its suggested ration by about one third. Afterward, the puppy may explore a bit more, or it may settle down for a nap. During the first four months of life, puppies need frequent rest and will exhibit great swings in energy levels—periods of great activity will be followed closely by periods of sound sleep.

The puppy will need its own sleeping area. While young, a small bed, sleeping box, or crate is recommended (see more on crates in Housebreaking on page 83). This area will be the pup's new "den," and it should return (or

be returned) to it for all sleeping. Bring the puppy to this area whenever it seems to be tiring. The sleeping area plays an important role in fostering a sense of security.

Although the crate may seem strikingly like a cage, your Siberian puppy will see it as his or her very own place. Do not let your own feelings become an obstacle to the use of this genuinely helpful training device.

Because puppies easily are overstimulated, try to make the first few days fun but not exhausting. This often is easier said than done with the exuberant Husky puppy. Everything is new and exciting, and the puppy may push itself beyond its endurance. Learning the voice and appearance of just the members of the immediate family is quite a chore for the puppy. Try not to bring a continuous stream of new faces to meet the new puppy. Introduce neighbors over the next few weeks or in short meetings while out for a walk. All meetings between young children in the household and the puppy should be closely monitored, and the children should be instructed on how to gently pet, lift, and handle a puppy.

Other Pets

Meeting the other pets in the home can be quite stressful for all involved. If possible, give the puppy a little time to adjust to the new surroundings before meeting other animals. Delaying this too long may unnerve the other pets, however, as they surely will sense the new presence. Make sure all the pets are strictly supervised and able to be restrained. Although adult Siberian Huskies rarely react aggressively toward puppies, anything can happen under such circumstances. Praise the animals highly throughout the meeting, showing the established pet lavish amounts of affection. If any animal should growl menacingly or lunge at the other, you immediately must correct with a stern warning and a shake of the neck, and remove it from the room. A new puppy is sometimes thought to be a threat to the household order, but this competitiveness usually eases with time.

Although a Siberian Husky is less likely to immediately go after a cat than many other breeds, there may be some aggressive behavior. Dogs and cats do not immediately understand each other's body language, and either animal's reactions can range from curiosity to apprehension to open hostility. A Husky that has been raised with cats generally will be peaceable toward them throughout its life. (My Reba always greeted each cat she met with a gentle nudge of the nose; this continued throughout her life despite more than a few scratches across the nose.)

Siberian Huskies are traditional pack animals used to living with several dogs. Occasionally, jealousy can be a problem in multidog households. Owners must try to give equal affection to all pets in the home to avoid competition and resentment. This is important especially when introducing a puppy, as it is easy to be so concerned with making the puppy feel wanted that the other pets feel neglected.

Children

Although Siberian Huskies are by nature loving toward children, some do not adapt well to the rough treatment children can inflict. For the safety of all concerned, a Husky should never be left alone with an infant. Even a docile dog such as this can be an imposing figure; just being stepped on can be dangerous to small children.

The First Night

Because puppies are not used to being alone, the first few nights may be frightening for them. Most will whimper or cry. It is important to establish a routine right from the start—the experience of the first few nights will set a pattern for the nights to come. Unless you plan on letting your dog sleep on your bed or in your room with you in the future, don't begin that pattern. Consistency is vital, and you shouldn't let the puppy do something one week that is forbidden the next.

Most puppies will need comforting during the first few nights, but do not overdo it. Bring the puppy to its sleeping area, pet it and talk soothingly to it for a few minutes, and then go.

This boy and his Husky puppy are sharing a special bonding moment.

Socialization classes introduce puppies to many situations and help produce well-mannered pups.

If you make it seem matter-of-fact, you will do more for the puppy than if you draw it out. If the puppy raises a fuss after a few minutes, return to reassure it. Do not linger there or remove it from the sleeping area. If you pick it up, the puppy will sense your uneasiness and learn that if it howls long enough you will come and get it. Soft, soothing background music or a hot water bottle under its blanket to imitate the mother's warmth often helps relieve the puppy's tension enough to let it fall asleep.

The puppy should settle down more easily over the next few nights. Remember to praise the puppy and lavish lots of attention on it first thing each morning to reward good behavior over night.

Daytime Care

To flourish, a Siberian Husky puppy will need lots of attention and companionship. It should not be expected to stay alone for more than short periods. Left alone for great lengths of time, a puppy will feel abandoned. Most maladjusted adults began as lonely or poorly treated puppies, and little can be done later to counteract the effects of a poor beginning. The end result often is a high-strung dog with undesirable habits, such as tension chewing, howling, or scratching. A Siberian Husky, in particular, does not do well when left to entertain itself.

When leaving the home for an extended time, try to arrange to take the puppy with you. If this is impossible, try to leave the dog with someone it is acquainted with. With modern work schedules, this often is not possible. Regardless, a puppy has exercise, elimination, and socialization needs that must be attended to during the day. As the dog matures, it will be able to be alone for longer periods; however, while a puppy, you may need to hire someone to care for it. In many cities there are professional dog walkers or sitters, and school-age children often are willing to come to your home and care for your pet. Huskies are people-oriented and rarely adapt well to extended separations. It is not fair to keep this breed if you cannot attend to this particular need.

Socialization

Puppy socialization classes, often called Kindergarten Puppy Training, are informative sessions held by local dog clubs to help introduce both owner and puppy to some basic training and discipline techniques. These classes do not include formal obedience training, but instead focus on showing owners some basic handling skills and housetraining methods.

The trainers also discuss such things as canine nutrition and health care and provide background information on how a puppy learns and understands. An emphasis is usually given on teaching the owner proper techniques for establishing his or her place as leader and gaining control over the puppy right from the start. A good trainer should evaluate each dog and base the lessons on what is shown by the animal. To communicate effectively, an owner must behave in a manner the puppy understands. If the dog does not receive the cues it expects from a leader, it will not feel compelled to obey. Puppy socialization classes help produce effective owners and well-mannered puppies.

Puppy socialization classes also are valuable because they expose the puppy to new people,

dogs, and surroundings. The dog's ability to know how to handle itself around other animals is vital. Siberian Huskies are peaceable by nature and rarely are antagonistic when encountering another dog. How the other dog will react is always an unknown, however, so the owner must be alert to recognize all possible dangers. Early lessons in socialization will help the dog to learn self-control and how to handle new situations. It is an owner's responsibility to ensure this proper behavior. Puppy socialization classes instill in the dog a sense of accomplishment and self-confidence, and these components are vital in developing a positive attitude toward training.

Outdoor Exercise and Housing

No breed enjoys the outdoors more than a Siberian Husky. They have flourished in some of the coldest, harshest areas on earth. Although most Siberian Huskies in the United States are kept as companions in the home, they also can adapt to being housed in a kennel building—provided there is plenty of human and canine companionship during the day. Siberians are much too people-oriented to be kept strictly as kennel dogs.

Siberian Huskies should be given plenty of time outdoors. They thrive when allowed to romp, and their quick bursts of speed are a sight to behold. Siberians run straight and fast, not in a circling pattern. They need adequate amounts of exercise to release tensions that may accumulate when confined indoors. The release they get from being outdoors keeps them more relaxed in the home and helps thwart such negative habits as tension chewing or howling.

A Doghouse

Siberian Huskies are very happy to spend a considerable amount of time outdoors. But no matter how hardy the breed and how impervious to the elements this breed seems, they still require proper protection from the elements. Doghouses can be constructed to provide adequate shelter against heat, cold, and dampness. It must be well insulated and large enough to let the dog fully stretch out, but not too large to lose warmth. The entrance should be just large enough to allow the dog to enter easily. A doghouse with a hinged top is easiest to clean.

The doghouse must be in a shaded area during the hot months and a sunny area during the cold months. It should be mounted on platform risers or placed on blocks to stand several inches off the ground so that there is no direct contact with the soil. Do not position the doghouse directly against a fence. Although Siberians are not noted climbers, they are good jumpers. Placing a doghouse in this way gives the dog the opportunity to climb on it and jump to freedom.

Fencing

Any area that Siberian Huskies are allowed to roam in freely must be properly fenced, preferably to a height of 5 or 6 feet (1.5–1.8 m). Huskies are easily distracted by the "call of the wild" and think they are impervious to any possible danger from passing vehicles. Because of these traits, it is extremely dangerous to allow them access to open areas. A secure run is a good solution, because it lets the dog roam but also keeps it in safe confinement. Siberians also like to dig, so the fence should be buried slightly to thwart any possible chance of tunneling under it. Most Siberians do not scheme to escape their surroundings, however. They dig for the thrill of digging and sometimes keep to their task until a hole large enough for lying down in has been devised.

Note: In some towns, laws have been enacted banning "vicious dogs," which potentially means any free-roaming dog. Check your town's rulings in regard to owning dogs. You will have to be zealous in making sure your dog never roams freely in a heavily populated neighborhood, as the dog will likely be impounded and possibly banned from returning to the home. Fines on owners deemed negligent often start at $100 and double with every incident.

Traveling with Siberians

Siberian Huskies love companionship and do not like staying home alone. They enjoy new situations, sights, and sounds; they do not enjoy solitude.

Traveling by Car

You should familiarize the dog with riding in the car from the time it is a puppy. The dog always should be placed in the back seat. Teach it to lie down or, preferably, to ride in its crate when the car is in motion. If your car is large enough to have open space at the back, you can purchase a dog grille to partition off an area for the dog. This keeps the dog from moving about and encourages it to settle down.

The car windows should be opened approximately 2 inches (5 cm) to improve air circulation during the ride. If you travel frequently without air-conditioning during hot weather, you can purchase specially designed window screens that allow more air to enter the window. When traveling during hot periods, your dog should receive a small amount of water at regular intervals to prevent dehydration. Make it a habit to bring an insulated container of cold water with you wherever you go. There are two important "nevers."

Never allow the dog to hang its head out the window while the car is in motion. This can result in eye, ear, and throat injuries.

Never leave a dog unattended in a parked car during the heat of the day. The temperature inside a parked car can soar in just minutes and can prove fatal to the dog. Puppies especially are susceptible to heatstroke.

If you are taking a trip of more than one hour, do not feed the dog for approximately four to six hours before leaving, as a full stomach can often lead to motion sickness. Withhold water two hours before the trip. If your

dog is highly excitable or prone to vomiting in the car and you are planning an extended ride, consult your veterinarian regarding possible medications. Tranquilizers should be used only when absolutely necessary, when prescribed by the veterinarian, as the primary effect of these drugs is to make the dog drowsy. They don't minimize the dog's physical discomfort and do, in fact, inhibit the dog's ability to regulate body temperature. Most dogs will outgrow a tendency toward motion sickness as they get more accustomed to trips in the car.

On extended trips, stop every two hours or so to let the dog relieve itself, have a drink, and get some exercise. It is especially important to remember to keep a Siberian Husky on leash during such stops.

Special arrangements and advance reservations may need to be made if your trip requires overnight lodging, because many facilities will not allow dogs. Your local automobile club or published travel guides may be able to give you a list of places near your destination that allow animals.

Bring an adequate supply of the dog's normal food on long trips. This helps reduce the chance of digestive problems. A traveling dog is faced already with many new and unusual conditions; having to switch to a new food is another chance to upset it.

Traveling by Plane

Traveling by airplane used to be a dangerous proposition for animals, as they were treated merely as cargo. In the last decade, however, regulations have been passed that greatly have

Make sure you give your Siberian Husky the outdoor time that it thrives on.

The beautiful Husky is a popular breed that needs proper care and attention.

improved air travel. All animals must now be better protected in flight and shielded from extremes of temperature. Traveling in airplanes has become commonplace for show dogs—many of which compete from coast to coast. Many breeders will have planned matings that involve partners from various areas of the country, making a quick airplane trip a necessity (usually for the bitch).

Because the space allotment for animals on an airplane is limited, be sure to make an advance reservation for the dog. Do your best to get the dog on a nonstop or at least direct

Pet carriers are a good idea when traveling with your dog.

flight. There is an added risk of the dog being misplaced or injured if it must be moved around to make connecting flights. If the dog must travel on connecting flights, arrange to break up the long trip with a rest stop.

If given proper notice, most airlines are able to furnish owners with suitable crates for shipping their dogs, for an additional charge. Dogs that are already accustomed to spending time in a crate will be less stressed than first-timers. If possible, allow a newcomer to try out the crate a few times before the actual trip.

Check with the airline prior to departure for instructions regarding how to board the dog. A health certificate issued within 30 days is required by most commercial airlines. To keep upsets to a minimum, the owner should also send a supply of the dog's normal food along on the trip.

The shipping crate should be marked clearly on the outside with "Live Animal," the dog's name, and the name, address, and phone number of both the sender and recipient. Tape another copy of this information *to the inside of the crate* with the dog.

You may want to place a blanket or some shredded newspaper at the bottom of the crate for a little added comfort for the dog. Enclose a nylon bone to help alleviate tension and boredom during the trip. Do not place food or water inside the crate before departure, as invariably it will spill and make the trip uncomfortable for the dog. You should, however, try to attach a water dish to the inside of the crate near the bars so that an attendant could pour water for the dog without having to open the crate, should the need arise. The dog must be exercised just before entering the crate.

Many novice shippers make the mistake of sedating their dogs before an air flight. Although it is true that a nervous dog can panic and injure itself during flight, it is better to teach the dog to relax in the crate rather than sedate it. Tranquilizers can depress respiration, and this factor—when combined with excessive heat and oxygen reduction, which are common conditions during air flight—can sometimes lead to heatstroke and death.

Withhold food for eight to ten hours before the flight, and be sure that the dog is exercised just prior to entering the crate. A soiled crate will make the dog very uncomfortable during the flight.

Stay with the crate for as long as possible. Notify every airline official connected with your flight that you have a dog being loaded. (I believe in being pesty when dealing with such valuable cargo!) Verify with airline officials that the dog has, indeed, been loaded on the plane before leaving the airport. If there is an extended delay or cancellation of the flight, you will want to be there to make new arrangements for the dog. You cannot be too careful when leaving your Husky in someone else's care.

Boarding Your Siberian

Occasionally, you will need to find good accommodations for your pet while you are away. Whatever method you use, always leave enough of the dog's normal food to last until your return. The best solution is, of course, to have someone the dog is familiar with take care of it. If this is impossible, ask the breeder from whom you purchased the dog to temporarily board it. The advantages of this are the familiarity he or she would have with the individual dog and the particular requirements and traits of Siberians. Because this breed needs a lot of human companionship, this may be a very beneficial arrangement for all concerned.

Boarding also is available at the facilities of some veterinarians or at commercial kennels.

These establishments are usually well managed, clean, and attentive to the dog's basic needs. Be sure to visit and inspect the kennel beforehand. Ask about the daily exercise routines and feeding procedures and check that it is accredited by the American Boarding Kennel Association (ABKA). You can expect to pay from $12 to $20 per day for this service. You can obtain a list of approved kennels in your area by writing the ABKA (see page 92 for the address).

Protecting Your Siberian

A sad side effect of popularity has been an increased number of Husky thefts. Several animal protection agencies have issued a warning that dognapping is on the increase. It may seem hard to imagine that a stranger would attempt to steal a Husky from its home or yard, but it does happen. Some dogs are more affable than others, and professional thieves often employ elaborate methods to restrain or entice a dog (such as parading a bitch in heat near an eager male). You can help protect your dog—and your neighborhood—by never leaving it unattended outside the home.

Although many owners believe that a tag on the dog's collar listing its name and the owner's name and address will suffice in helping the dog find its way home should it somehow stray, this protection is limited. The collar could be torn off by the dog or purposely removed by a thief. There are two more reliable sources to identify and find your missing dog: microchip implantation and tattooing.

Microchips

A high-tech method of identification is becoming quite popular. A tiny microchip containing information on the dog and its medical history is injected just under the skin at the base of the dog's neck. The injection procedure is painless for the animal and the chip is embedded permanently. A hand-held scanner placed over the chip will retrieve the microchip's information, which then can be decoded by a computer at the central registry that records the specific information on the dog. Most humane society shelters and veterinarians now have scanners, which are being used to identify a higher percentage of lost animals each year and return them to their owners. The procedure is relatively inexpensive, and there is a nominal annual renewal fee to keep the dog's information on file in the national registry.

Tattooing

It is also a good idea to have your Siberian Husky tattooed. This relatively painless procedure can be performed by most veterinarians for a nominal fee. Many dog clubs also hold annual clinics to perform this service for dog owners. The use of tattoos is endorsed by dog organizations, and show competitors are not penalized for having a tattoo.

The tattoo will be a permanent aid for identifying the dog should it become lost. It also will prevent the dog from being sold to research laboratories that sometimes purchase strays.

In most cases, the dog's AKC registration number or the owner's social security number is tattooed onto the dog's inner thigh. Although the inside of the ear can also be used, there have been cases where a dog's ear has been cut off to remove the tattoo. The tattoo number should then be listed with one of the national registries, which will record for an annual fee all pertinent information.

FEEDING SIBERIAN HUSKIES

What you feed your dog will have a direct impact on its overall health and longevity. Your task is to select a food that is complete nutritionally and balanced and suited to your dog's particular lifestyle. Most popular brands available in the local supermarket or from pet shops and suppliers are the end result of many years of research into canine nutrition. An owner should still do a bit of comparative shopping and label reading before deciding on a brand, as the most popular dog food may not be the best food for your Siberian Husky.

Types of Food

What type of food is best for your Siberian Husky? There are several possible answers. Some owners use only one type, whereas others use a combination. The task is to present a daily ration that is nutritionally complete and balanced and suited to your dog's particular lifestyle. Which type of food is best? Which brand is best? The owner must consider many factors and then do some comparative shopping when making this decision.

Dry Food

Ounce for ounce dry food is the least expensive type, and, accordingly, is the most commonly used. There can be great variation in the

Siberian Huskies are usually eager eaters. The owner must provide nutritious meals.

quality of dry foods, however. Dry foods are composed of 8 to 10 percent water, with the remaining ingredients being various cereals, soy, meat by-products, and small amounts of fats, vitamins, and minerals.

Buy only those brands labeled "nutritionally complete;" however, keep in mind that this label is not the only determining factor you should check. Some dry products require the dog to eat an excessive amount of the food to fulfill daily dietary needs. Various products' intake requirements can be determined by examining the suggested feeding amounts per weight of dog as listed on the package. A dry food that is priced low may, in the long run, be more expensive than other brands because the dog needs to eat more of it to obtain all the benefits from the food. Also, when large amounts of food must be ingested, there will be an inevitable increase in excreted waste materials. A slight variation of content may be observed from batch to batch in many dry food products, as fluctuations in the availability of the base crop (soy, corn, barley) produce a slightly different blending at various times during the year.

The meat-meal based dry foods used by most commercial breeders and sold in pet shops and supply houses offer a stable mixture from batch to batch that nutritionally is complete, easily digested, and contains enough fiber to help produce a firm stool. In addition, the feeding amounts needed to fulfill all

CHECKLIST

Rules for Feeding

The following basic rules may help protect your Husky from feeding-related problems.

✔ Supply ample amounts of clean, fresh water at all times, especially in hot weather.

✔ Wash all food and water bowls daily in hot, soapy water to prevent bacterial growth.

✔ Maintain a constant diet, as sudden changes may cause digestive upset.

✔ Introduce new foods slowly, in modest amounts mixed in with the food the dog is accustomed to.

✔ Bring an ample supply of the dog's usual food when traveling or when the dog must be kenneled.

✔ Take up the water bowl at night if the dog is having problems with housebreaking.

✔ Serve leftover canned food at room temperature.

nutritional requirements do not force the dog to overeat. These products may cost a bit more on a per pound basis, but the superior quality is worth the added expense.

Dry food products are low in fat content and may be insufficient for an active dog, such as the Siberian Husky. This easily is compensated for by adding approximately one-half can of canned food or several tablespoons of cottage cheese to the kibble as a supplement.

Canned Food

Ounce for ounce, canned dog food is very expensive, considering most contain more than 75 percent water. The remaining portion is composed of meat by-products, soy fillers, vitamins, minerals, and, frequently, artificial coloring and preservatives. The high water level and additives often have a diuretic effect on many dogs, resulting in housebreaking problems.

The canned food products designed for the various stages of life are most recommended. Canned food should comprise no more than one quarter of the daily intake and should be combined with a high-quality dry food for best results. Few dogs dislike canned food, so this is a recommended food for dogs needing to gain or maintain weight. Conversely, it is the food to withhold first for overweight dogs.

Semimoist Food

Semimoist foods are usually packaged in pouches or shaped as hamburgers. They are composed primarily of soy meal, meat by-products, and cereal, and contain approximately 25 percent water. This food is very expensive and contains a considerable amount of additives and preservatives. Although the levels of sugar and salt have decreased recently, semimoist products are still very high in calories. Some dogs have had allergic reactions to the preservatives contained in the highly processed semimoist food. This allergy can range from hyperactivity to skin biting or scratching in sensitive dogs.

Home Cooked Meals

If you want to raise a dog strictly on home prepared meals, it is advisable that you do so under the supervision of a veterinarian or nutritionist. You are competing against the products of pet food companies that have spent millions of dollars specifically on canine nutrition research. Most pet households are well served by commercial products. However, a breeder knows best the needs of his or her dogs. Siberian Huskies used in dogsled racing certainly would need a specialized diet containing high levels of carbohydrates for energy and fats to stave off the effects of continued exposure to cold weather, but this supplementation is done in specific amounts at specific times, using their own blend of kibble, meat, and supplements—being sure the end result is nutritionally complete.

Interested fanciers and homes with more than one Siberian Husky might save some money by devising an individual blend of kibble, meat, vegetables, and cottage cheese. Although this may be effective for lowering the monthly food expense, the primary concern should be nutrition, not saving pennies.

Supplements

Table scraps can be too much of a good thing for your dog. Although Reba undoubtedly will love those fatty meat scraps, the end result may be a case of diarrhea. Small amounts of fruits, vegetables, and cereals will, in fact, promote proper digestion. Hard or crunchy foods, such as carrots or a sturdy knucklebone, can keep the teeth clean by scraping away tartar along the tooth surface.

Be very selective with bones, however, as these can be constipating and potentially deadly should an improper bone splinter when chewed. Sturdy nylon bones are safest and can

be purchased in pet shops, supermarkets, and specialty stores. Although dogs certainly love rawhide bones, they have been linked to intestinal blockage in some dogs, so these should be given sparingly and while the dog is under surveillance. Remove any unfinished portions when you are not around to monitor the dog.

Aside from nursing mothers, few Siberian Huskies will need vitamin supplements. Vitamin deficiencies are rare and should not occur if a dog is healthy and eating a quality diet. It especially is important not to oversupplement growing puppies, because there can be serious side effects from excessive vitamin intake. A well-balanced diet and an adequate amount of exercise should be all your Siberian Husky needs to stay in good health.

The Feeding Process

Siberian Huskies are eager eaters. They usually clean their bowls quickly and, if satisfied, move off in search of adventure. Few Huskies would put eating ahead of play, if given the chance, so feeding must be supervised and regulated. Wise owners must find the blend that works best for their dog.

Where to Feed

All dogs have pack instincts, and they should be allowed adequate time and space to eat their meal in an out-of-the-way place rather than in the middle of the kitchen at the busiest time of day. If left to eat in a high-traffic area, a dog may worry whether its food is going to be taken away, and it may develop some bad habits in response. An anxious dog may quickly devour its food. This could lead to digestive problems or

vomiting. In the worst case, a dog that gulps its food can develop a digestive condition called bloat, where the stomach swells after filling with gas and fluids, often twisting and becoming an immediate life-threatening situation.

Buy a high-quality food appropriate for your dog's stage of life.

An anxious dog might also become overprotective of its food. This habit cannot be tolerated, as your Husky must be trained from an early age to allow you to pick up and remove its food, if necessary, without protest. Occasionally moving the bowl to various places in a room will keep the dog from getting too routinized and will promote healthy eating patterns.

When to Feed

The owner's daily routine and the age of the dog are the main factors in deciding when to feed the dog each day. Puppies may need several small meals a day, because they

Water is an important part of your dog's diet, no matter what its age.

Puppies usually need several small meals throughout the day.

cannot physically handle large amounts of food. If possible, puppies should be allowed to eat when hungry, in a free choice system. This situation is often impossible in a multidog household, as the older dogs will certainly clear any leftovers, in which case three meals usually will suffice. At approximately nine months of age, only two daily meals will be necessary. The adult feeding pattern usually consists of either one large meal a day, generally in the late afternoon or at night, or two smaller meals daily.

How Much to Feed

No definite formula exists for determining how much food one dog will need daily. The

Provide your dog with the appropriate toys for chewing.

dog's appetite will be the natural guide, as Huskies rarely eat more than they need. The amount listed on the label is a guide—every dog has a different metabolism and lifestyle. Working Siberian Huskies require more calories each day than an older, less active dog. Growing puppies and pregnant or lactating bitches will need a special diet high in protein and calories. Dogs that spend a good deal of time outside during cold weather will require extra calories, usually in the form of supplementary fats, to help them cope with the weather.

Keep the feeding process simple. The dog should have some privacy and ample time to eat its meal (generally 15 to 20 minutes). Pick up and discard any food that remains after this time. You should adjust the amount slightly at the next meal if the dog has been leaving food uneaten, until the dog clears its bowl. If the bowl is quickly emptied, increase the amount slightly until the dog is satisfied.

Problem Eaters

Should the dog refuse its food, discard what remains and do not offer a replacement until the next scheduled meal. By catering to the demands of a picky eater you enhance, rather than solve, the problem. If the dog appears hungry and healthy and still continues to turn away from its food, change what you are feeding it *one time* and see if the dog only had an aversion to the food you have been giving. Some dog food companies change the contents of their product slightly from batch to batch, so the dog may dislike the current batch. However, Siberian Huskies rarely are problem eaters. A sudden lack of interest in eating usually is caused by a health or behavioral problem. If the

problem persists for more than a few meals, the dog should be examined by a veterinarian.

If there is no physical reason for this lack of appetite, chalk it up to stubbornness. Few dogs will continue this for long once they see that you will not give in. Never whine or plead with the dog to eat. You will either convince the dog that there really is something wrong with the food (why else would my master be carrying on about it?) or it will sense your insecurity and exploit it.

Teething and Chewing

A Siberian Husky will chew while teething, so owners should be aware and prepare for it. A puppy has a strong urge to chew between four and ten months of age, but don't be fooled into thinking it will all end in a few months. The need to chew will remain as the dog matures.

The best method to rid accumulated tartar buildup on the teeth (short of a professional scraping or ultrasonic cleaning) is by chewing hard substances. Because there is little of this in the diet, other objects must be found. Some dogs also chew to release tension, often causing extensive and expensive damage to household goods. A Siberian Husky left alone for long stretches would be a prime candidate.

No simple, foolproof method exists to stop dogs from chewing. Each Husky will come up with its own "hit list." The best course is prevention. Give the dog an ample supply of suitable chew objects, and let it know exactly what *may* and *may not* be chewed. Do not give the dog an old slipper as a chew toy and then expect it to leave the rest of your shoes alone. Although most dogs enjoy rawhide bones,

Siberian Huskies usually can devour them quickly, and rawhide has been linked to intestinal blockage. Nylon bones are long lasting and sturdy, but many dogs don't like them. Hard beef or veal bones, such as from the knuckle, should be given only occasionally, as they can be constipating and abrasive to tooth enamel. Plastic toys should only be given when the dog is being supervised, as these can be torn apart and swallowed, leading to choking.

While the dog is teething it will need to chew. To keep losses to a minimum, confine the dog when it cannot be supervised and always have a suitable chew toy available. The need to chew will continue even after the first teeth are shed. There may be another intense bout with chewing when the back molars are emerging at around eight or nine months of age.

Unfortunately, learning to deal with teething is a trial-and-error process. If you give your dog access to all areas of your house, you may discover that your Husky has developed a taste for your book collection or venetian blinds. If you catch the dog with a forbidden object in its mouth, immediately remove it from the dog's clutches, shake it in front of the dog's head and tap it as you say *"No!"* in a stern voice. This will help the dog to connect your displeasure with its chewing of the object. If the dog continues chewing, add a quick but nonviolent shake of the neck to your correction. This is intended to shock the dog, not injure it. Replace the forbidden object with something that the dog is allowed to chew.

Chewing can be fatal for the dog should it ever bite on an electric cord. An inquisitive puppy often will mouth wires, so be sure to secure them during your puppy-proofing of the household. Many plants are poisonous if ingested, and dogs often are attracted to them by their smell or appearance. If you have poisonous plants in the household (such as poinsettia, dieffenbachia, or foxglove), place them out of the puppy's reach.

GROOMING SIBERIAN HUSKIES

Coat Care

The Siberian Husky is a double-coated breed. This means that it has a woolly undercoat that serves as the dog's insulation against cold or heat, and a layer of longer, harsher outercoat that grows through the undercoat. Shedding will occur at least once a year in males and twice a year (generally spring and fall) in females. High humidity or excessive heat often will make the shedding worse. Because the amount of hair shed by a Siberian is fairly substantial, this should be kept in mind when deciding to purchase this breed.

The shedding process usually will take from three to six weeks, with a new coat growing in during the next three to four months. During the active shedding period, groom the dog daily. Between shedding times, regular brushing will remove excess loose hairs. If you maintain a weekly grooming pattern, you should not be plagued continually by hair left behind wherever the dog has been, as is common with some other long-haired breeds.

The main goal of grooming is to remove dead hairs that are clinging to the coat. In the process, you are also cleaning the skin and the shafts of the living hair. The main tools for grooming the Siberian Husky are a wide-toothed comb and a bristle brush. The tips of

Siberian Huskies have double coats and they tend to shed substantially.

the comb's teeth must always be rounded, and the bristles of the brush must be long enough to reach through the coat to the skin. The Siberian's coat is not to be cut or trimmed—ever. Very minor tidying of stray hairs may occur around such areas as the feet in show dogs, but any shaping or stripping of the Siberian's coat is unwarranted.

The comb should be used to run through the coat to break up any mats or snags and to remove the dead hairs. Knots should be worked out a little at a time, using the comb and the fingers to gently tease the hairs apart. It is especially important to comb through the undercoat during shedding. A fine-toothed comb is handy for the areas under the chin and tail and between the ears. Use the brush once the combing is complete to finish off the coat. Brush the coat forward, over the head and shoulders, before combing it back. Brush the rear areas in the direction of the lay of the coat. Extra attention should be given to the hindquarters, as guard hairs in this area often accumulate into mats.

Because Siberians are susceptible to skin allergies, be sure to have a veterinarian check the coat if you notice any excessive scratching or biting at the skin.

Bathing

The Siberian Husky will not need bathing more than twice a year, usually in the spring and fall, coinciding with the molting of the coat. The Husky's coat remains clean year-round and should not take on a "doggy" odor.

When bathing is needed, use a very mild soap designed especially for dogs—not products for humans, because they are too harsh and drying for a dog's hair. Wet the dog thoroughly, working the water down through the undercoat to the skin. Begin with the head and proceed down, being very careful that water and shampoo do not get into the dog's eyes and ears. Once the dog is lathered fully, rinse the coat well with lots of warm water. The soap must be removed totally from the undercoat or else the skin may become irritated and the dog may develop dandruff.

Towel the dog down, and do not let it be exposed to any cool air until the undercoat is dried totally. A hair dryer set on low may be

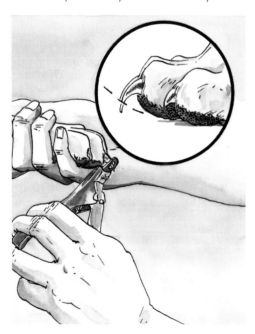

used to speed the drying process. Once dry, give the dog a complete grooming to be sure that no mats have formed.

Nail Care

Siberian Huskies rarely are sedentary dogs. Quite the contrary, they thrive on time outdoors and activity. Although most Huskies get enough exposure to rough pavement to keep their nails naturally worn down, owners still should inspect the nails regularly to ensure that they do not need to be trimmed. Overgrown nails can impede the normal placement of the foot and affect a dog's gait.

Most dogs naturally are reluctant to have their feet held for any time. To counteract this instinct to pull away, regularly touch and play with its feet and toes while petting and grooming to indoctrinate the puppy to having this area touched. You can later try massaging the footpads. This will prepare the dog should the nails ever need a clipping.

A specially designed guillotine clipper, which can be purchased from pet stores, grooming shops, and veterinarians, should be used to trim the nails. If you are inexperienced, have your veterinarian show you this simple procedure. Once you are instructed, this process can be handled at home when required.

Cut only the outer shell of the nail, as cutting too close to the vein (called the "quick") is quite painful for the dog and can cause bleeding. Once shortened to its proper length,

When trimming your pet's nails, be sure to cut the nail on a slight angle, as shown. Cut only the outer shell of the nail to avoid the "quick," which will bleed if cut.

smooth the surface of the nail with a few brushes of an emery board. If you cut too close to the quick and the nail bleeds, apply pressure to the area by holding a piece of cotton gauze over the nail or use a styptic pencil. Once the bleeding stops, dab the nail with a mild antiseptic.

Foot Care

Siberian Huskies make great use of their legs and feet, which makes them very susceptible to various minor injuries. The pads of the feet should be inspected regularly, especially if the dog limps or favors a leg. Burrs, splinters, or stones can become embedded in and between the pads of the foot, and scratches and cuts on the pad are common. For minor problems, a gentle cleaning, using sterilized tweezers to remove any objects and a mild antiseptic, should work effectively.

If the dog suddenly acquires a limp and favors or licks one foot, it may have been stung by an insect. If this is the case, apply an ice compress to reduce or prevent swelling and ease the pain. Unless there is an allergic reaction of some sort (see Stinging Insects, page 62), this discomfort should pass quickly.

If there is no evidence of a cut or sting, and the dog still indicates pain in the foot, there may be an injury to the bones or muscle tissue or there may be an object deeply embedded in the footpad. Although Siberian Huskies generally can run at full speed for an extended time, occasionally they may turn too sharply or strain to pull too much weight and suffer muscle pulls. Although rarely serious, these conditions require the expertise of a veterinarian.

During the winter, your Husky's feet may be exposed to chemicals that are placed on the sidewalks to melt ice and snow. These compounds can be caustic to a dog's footpads and skin. If the dog has walked on these chemicals, rinse its feet with warm, soapy water once it returns home. If the dog's pads appear sensitive to the touch, apply a thin layer of petroleum jelly to soothe them. If these chemicals are not removed, the dog may try to alleviate the discomfort by licking them. Ingesting such poisonous materials can be hazardous to the dog's digestive tract.

A Siberian Husky's undercoat provides insulation from the cold.

Grooming removes dead hairs that cling to your Husky's coat.

Evaluating Your Dog's Condition

A quick inspection of your dog performed during its routine grooming sessions is a good way to observe its overall health. Start by running your hands over the dog's entire body and feeling for anything unusual, such as cuts, swelling, cysts, or areas that cause the dog pain when touched. Be sure to get your fingers through the double coat and down to the skin to look and feel for signs of irritation. You should then turn to the head and begin a more thorough evaluation.

Being outdoors-loving dogs, Siberian Huskies have a high potential for minor abrasions and irritations, especially on the feet, legs, eyes, and ears.

Eyes

A slight discharge in the corner of the eyes is quite normal and can be cleared away easily with a damp, lint-free cloth. Do not use cotton balls because they can leave behind tiny fibers in the eye. A clear discharge usually is related to the drainage of the tears or minor irritations and inflammations, such as conjunctivitis. Consult your veterinarian if this discharge becomes excessive or changes to a cloudy or yellowish color, or if the dog blinks constantly and the eye is red.

An active Siberian Husky may get a minor scratch on the eye when running through the underbrush. This scratch should heal quickly without any special attention. If a burr or small object gets into the eye, irrigate the eye with some warm water or carefully dab the corner with a soft cloth. If it becomes lodged, seek immediate veterinary care, as probing for it may seriously injure the eye. A constant discharge or a pawing of the area requires a veterinary inspection.

Ears

With dogs such as Siberian Huskies, the ears can get scratched and irritated quite easily. A dog with ear problems constantly will shake its head or rub its ears with its paws or on the ground. If there is an excessive amount of visible earwax, redness, swelling, or a foul odor coming from the ear canal, a veterinarian's attention is required.

Simple abrasions are the most common ear irritation. The most important task is to keep the afflicted area clean to avoid infection. If you find an abrased area or mild scratches, your veterinarian can advise you regarding treatment.

Never probe down into the dog's ear canal, as this can be extremely painful and can cause great damage. To help remove the normal accumulation of wax and dirt in the outer ear, swab the easily accessible areas of the ear

During a routine examination the veterinarian will inspect your dog's ear canal for any excessive buildup or signs of infection.

with a cotton ball wet with a little warm water. Ointments made specially for cleaning the ear can be purchased from pet shops, grooming parlors, or your veterinarian if cleanliness is a continual problem. Avoid oily compounds, because they may attract and retain dirt.

If you suspect that the inner ear is clogged with wax, bring the dog to your veterinarian for a thorough cleaning. If the problem is chronic, ask your veterinarian for instructions on how to perform this procedure at home.

If the dog winces with pain when its ears are touched, an infection may be present. An inflammation of the ear, termed otitis, can be treated topically or systemically, depending on the causative agent. This condition can have several causes, such as parasitic mites or a bacterial or yeast infection. Because an accurate diagnosis is required, seek veterinary assistance at the onset of the problem.

Tooth Care

Tartar can be a lifelong problem for dogs. A diet that includes items naturally abrasive to the teeth (such as carrots) can help keep teeth clean. Chewing a safe, hard bone will help remove most buildup.

Accustoming your Husky from puppyhood to having its teeth gently cleaned with a soft child's toothbrush or moistened gauze pad will ease your task in later years when the teeth require more cleaning. A yellowing of the tooth exterior is common as the dog ages and often can be minimized by routine treatment. The teeth can be brushed once or twice a week with a mild paste of baking soda and hydrogen peroxide to remove most stain and plaque.

If discoloring remains despite weekly brushings, the teeth may need to be scaled by your veterinarian. If the buildup is chronic, your vet-

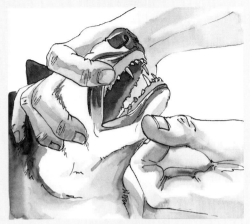

Check your dog's teeth regularly for signs of tartar buildup. If severe, the tartar will need to be removed by your veterinarian.

erinarian can show you how to perform this scaling at home as part of the dog's regular grooming process.

Many tooth problems are not revealed by the outward condition or color of the teeth. A sudden change in the dog's breath that lasts for more than a few days may indicate a problem with either the teeth or the throat. A loss of appetite could stem from decayed teeth, which make it painful for the dog to eat. Inspect the teeth and gums for any obvious sign of infection, swelling, bleeding, or sensitivity to the touch. An abscessed tooth sometimes manifests itself as a boil-like growth on the cheek area. Your veterinarian should be informed as soon as you notice any of these conditions.

Occasional bad breath can be treated with several commercial products, which the dog chews and ingests. Most contain chlorophyll, which is a natural ingredient that helps promote fresh breath.

SAFEGUARDING YOUR DOG'S HEALTH

Veterinary Care

Regardless of your Siberian Husky's outward condition, it should get an annual physical examination from your veterinarian. At this time, he or she will evaluate the dog's general condition, test for internal parasites, and determine if the dog needs any injections.

Any dog that shows symptoms of illness, weight loss, or abnormal behavior (such as drinking excessive amounts of water) should be taken to a veterinarian shortly after noticing the problem. Delaying treatment can be a costly mistake. Many illnesses that are treated easily in the early stages can become life-threatening if treatment is delayed.

Basic Health Care

There are several simple procedures that every pet owner should know and some that are best left to health care professionals.

Taking the Temperature

The first is taking a dog's temperature. Lubricate the end of a heavy-duty rectal thermometer with a little petroleum or KY jelly. As a safety precaution, you may want to have an assistant help restrain the dog during the

Preventive health care begins in puppyhood and continues throughout the dog's life.

insertion so that the dog does not inadvertently sit down or otherwise break the thermometer. It is best to have the dog stand, but it can also lie on its side. One person should get a secure grasp on the dog while the other lifts the tail and inserts the thermometer. To get an accurate reading, the thermometer should remain for one to two minutes. A dog's normal temperature is slightly higher than a human's—100 to 102°F (37.7–38.9°C) is normal.

Giving Medication

Most dog owners will have to give their pet medication at one time or another. Although giving a dog a pill or capsule may seem like a simple enough procedure, most dogs quickly master the technique for not swallowing pills and defiantly spit them right out. The easiest method is to disguise the pill in something tasty, such as a small chunk of liverwurst or hamburger or a piece of cheese. If your dog is not so easily tricked, gently pry the dog's mouth open by applying pressure at the back of its mouth, tilt the heat up *slightly,* and insert the pill as far back on the tongue as possible. Close the jaws and watch for a swallow. Gently stroking the throat may help. *Never lift the dog's head straight up and drop in the pill; in this position, the pill can be inhaled into the windpipe rather than swallowed.*

The best way to administer liquid medicine is to place it in a medicine spoon or syringe and

When giving your dog a pill, apply gentle pressure at the back of the mouth to open it.

until you are sure it has swallowed or else the dog may easily spit the medicine out. Again, never hold the head in an exaggerated upward position, as this invites choking.

Although some liquid and powdered medicines may be mixed into the dog's food (check with your veterinarian first), many dogs smell or taste the additives right away and won't eat the food. If this is the case, powdered medications usually can be liquefied by adding a little water, and you can proceed as described above.

Monitoring the Heart

A dog's heartbeat also can be monitored easily. Although a Siberian Husky's normal heartbeat is 60 to 90 beats per minute, it may vary because of factors such as age, temperature, exertion, stress, and illness. A pulse can be found in the front paw, but the one located on the inside of the thigh is the easiest to take. Press softly against the pulse and monitor the pattern and rate of the beats. This procedure should be performed if you ever notice signs of extreme fatigue, fainting, or hyperactivity in your dog. Any abnormal patterns in the heartbeat require immediate attention by a veterinarian.

pour it into the *back of the mouth* by lifting up the side of the dog's lower lip by the back molars and holding the head *slightly* upward. This method lets the medicine slide down the throat. Keep a grasp around the dog's muzzle

Monitoring Breathing

You should also be aware of your dog's normal rate of breathing. When relaxed, the breathing should be easy and smooth—from 10 to 30 breaths per minute.

Continue by tilting the head up slightly and inserting the pill at the back of the tongue. Close the mouth and wait to see a swallow.

Vaccinations

Most puppies receive their first immunizations while still with their breeder. These initial vaccinations are for distemper, hepatitis, leptospirosis, and parvovirus at around six to eight weeks. Follow-up shots will be required for most vaccines, on a schedule devised by your veterinarian (generally every three weeks until the initial boosters are finished). A rabies vaccination also will be needed, as well as boosters as the dog matures. By keeping the required vaccinations and boosters current, you can protect your dog from many infectious diseases. Get the records of your dog's earliest shots from the breeder and give this information to your veterinarian. Ask the breeder if the dog has been tested or treated for worms. If it has, find out what type of worm the dog was infected with, what medication was used to treat it, and how the dog reacted to the medication. Worms are very common in puppies, and this background information can be very helpful.

Parasites

Outdoor-loving dogs such as Siberian Huskies are often in contact with contaminations that can produce parasite infections. The owner should closely watch the dog's condition so that problems can be caught in the initial stages. This vigilance is especially important in the warm months, when infestations are more prevalent.

Heartworm is spread when a mosquito bites an infected animal and transfers the parasite to another unprotected host. As the worms mature they lodge in the dog's heart where they can do great damage.

Worms

Although worms are very common in dogs (especially puppies), they should never be ignored. Severe worm infestations can be very debilitating and sometimes life-threatening. Diagnosing the type of worm and selecting the proper medication is a job only for a veterinarian. Routine wormings using over-the-counter preparations are unnecessary and can be dangerous.

Symptoms of worm infestation include weight loss, weakness, a bloated stomach, diarrhea, dull coat, loss of appetite, or, alternatively, a voracious appetite. The dog may drag its anus across the ground or lick and bite around the tail area. In some cases, segments of worms may cling to the dog's feces and be visible on cleanup. Some infected dogs will give little outward sign of the problem until heavily infested, which highlights the importance of having the dog routinely checked for worms.

Detecting the presence of most worms is done by microscopic examination of stool or blood samples. The most common types of worm are the roundworm, tapeworm, hookworm, and heartworm. Each requires a specific medicine. In the case of heartworm (a disease primarily spread by mosquitoes), once the dog has been shown by blood test to be free of the parasite, a *preventive* medication in the form of a pill or chew treat can be administered on a monthly basis throughout mosquito season (early spring until after a killing frost) to keep the dog free from infection. Many owners prefer to keep the dog on this medication year-round, as this will avoid having to have the dog's blood tested again at the start of the next mosquito season. There are also pills available that combine heartworm protection with

Make sure that your dog has current raccinations and booster shots.

medication that will prevent flea infestation by breaking the flea life cycle at the egg stage (see below).

Fleas

Fleas can make a dog's life miserable. They invade the host, bite its skin, suck its blood, itch unbearably, and sometimes infect the dog with tapeworm. The severity of the problem usually depends on the local climate and the diligence of the owner in detecting and ridding them from the dog and its housing. Because of their double coats, Siberian Huskies may harbor fleas and skin irritations that are not seen easily, so owners must routinely inspect the dog's

Tapeworm eggs are ingested by fleas and hatch in the fleas' intestines. If a dog ingests an infected flea, the tapeworms mature in the dog's intestines and lay eggs that are passed in the dog's stool.

skin, especially if the dog is scratching or biting itself. Left unchecked, an afflicted dog can tear out layer and layer of coat and ultimately bloody its skin trying to relieve the itching.

The best way to control fleas is to prevent them by giving the dog a monthly dose of Lufenuron, which is marketed under several product names. Once in the bloodstream, the medicine is ingested by the flea whenever it bites the dog. The medicine interrupts the flea's reproduction cycle by preventing it from producing viable eggs. However, the medicine will not kill adult fleas, so it will take several weeks to take effect on an already infected animal. Because it causes stomach upset in some animals the pill should be given with a meal. This treatment is also relatively expensive, costing more than $70 per year.

Another preventive measure is to put a liquid insecticide into the dog's coat before infestation. This chemical is applied along the dog's back and tail and then combed through the coat. It must be reapplied at regular intervals. Although this procedure is not inexpensive, it has been highly effective for many dogs.

Despite your best efforts, if your dog does get a minor infestation, you can attempt to remove the fleas "naturally" by thoroughly brushing the dog's coat using a flea comb. This comb has thin blades that expose the fleas when you glide the comb along the skin. With the Siberian's thick coat and undercoat, this is all but impossible. Most owners use the pow-

ders and sprays designed specifically to kill fleas. They can be purchased at pet stores or grooming shops. The coat must be doused thoroughly with the repellent for it to work, and the active ingredient must reach the skin. Be extremely careful when applying the material. Cover the dog's eyes, nose, mouth, and ears, and slowly work the insecticide into the coat, working against the grain.

For heavy infestations, a flea dip bath will be needed. Many grooming parlors will do this, or you can do it at home. Always use products designed just for this purpose, and read all directions before beginning.

Once the dog has been ridded of fleas, you will have to ensure that the house, especially the dog's bedding, also is free of parasites and eggs. If the fleas are in the household carpeting, a heavy-duty insect bomb (available at most hardware stores and pet shops) will destroy all the breeding colonies.

A flea collar can provide a measure of protection from reinfection, but its powers are limited. Be sure to remove the collar if it gets wet, because it can become irritating to the skin.

Ticks

Ticks are another common problem that should not be taken lightly. They are disease carriers and can be painful for the afflicted dog. Once on their host, they gnaw through the skin and implant themselves so that they can suck and live off the dog's blood. One variety of tick, the deer tick, can induce Lyme disease in dogs as well as other animals and humans. If left untreated, this disease leads to arthritis, severe headaches, and heart problems.

Ticks are not detected easily on Siberian Huskies, because they are merely a fraction of an inch when they enter the dog's coat. Although flea and tick collars may help repel the parasite, they are only effective around the neck area. Infestations commonly occur on the hindquarters and around the ears.

A tick must be removed carefully. If simply ripped from the skin, the tick's head can tear away from the body and remain embedded in the skin, resulting in an infection or abscess. The proper way to remove a tick is to grasp it firmly using tweezers placed close to the skin. Wear protective gloves to minimize human exposure to such conditions as Lyme disease. Apply firm but gentle upward pressure. *Do not twist.* An alternative is to apply a tick dip, which can be purchased from most veterinarians or pet shops. This will, in effect, suffocate the tick and make it release its hold on the dog's skin. *Never try to burn a tick off with a match or a cigarette.* The dangers of this should be evident. Once a tick has been removed, a small lump or swollen area may remain for several days.

Lice and Mites

Several other types of external parasites can attack a dog, especially during the warm summer months. Lice or mite infestations are common and can result in uncontrollable itching and scratching in afflicted dogs. Because this can cause extensive damage to the dog's coat and skin that may take a long time to heal, it is important to catch skin problems in the early stages. If you notice any clusters of eggs, a rash of bumps, or pustules on the skin, consult your veterinarian for a proper diagnosis and treatment.

Stinging Insects

Bee and insect bites are difficult to detect. Many dogs will snap at a passing bee, oftentimes suffering the consequences. If you happen to witness your dog being bitten, or if you notice a sudden onset of limping, check the site and see if a stinger is still embedded. If it is, carefully remove it by scraping your fingernail or the side of a credit card across the base of the bite using a scooping motion. This will remove the stinger and limit the spread of the venom. If possible, apply ice or a cold compress to reduce swelling.

Whereas an insect bite usually will be little more than a momentary discomfort for the dog, occasionally a dog will have an allergic reaction to a bite. Reactions will vary from dog to dog, depending on level of sensitivity. A case of hives or localized swelling generally will subside in a matter of hours, with no lasting effect. A more severe reaction, such as marked swelling or difficulty in breathing, requires immediate veterinary attention. For most cases, administering an over-the-counter antihistamine (as advised by your veterinarian) or a corticosteroid will relieve most symptoms. If your dog is allergic to stinging insects, consult with your veterinarian and devise a strategy for coping with future emergencies and have an antidote readily available at all times.

Common Health Problems

Siberian Huskies are adaptable to all types of weather and terrain. During their lives, most dogs will contract a few minor illnesses, and most of these should be no more serious than the passing upsets most humans must endure. However, because dogs cannot communicate their discomforts, it is the owner's responsibility to monitor the dog's condition and make a decision about whether veterinary attention is required.

Diarrhea

A mild case of diarrhea may have many causes—most of which are not serious or life-threatening. The first step in treating this condition is to remove food from the dog for the next 12 to 24 hours to allow the dog's digestive system to rid itself of any offending material. A small amount of water or a tablespoon of Kaopectate is permissible. If symptoms do not worsen during the next 24 hours, the dog can be given several small, bland meals containing a binding agent, such as rice or oatmeal.

If you notice a bloody discharge or if the diarrhea continues for more than 48 hours, veterinary assistance is needed. Diarrhea combined with vomiting and/or a high fever can be symptomatic of a serious problem, so do not delay in getting help if the dog's condition seems to worsen.

Vomiting

Vomiting is caused by various illnesses that involve the digestive tract. Most incidents are quick to pass and often are related to something the dog has eaten or to viruses. Severe, continued vomiting is very serious, however, and can lead to dehydration.

If the vomiting is limited to only a few episodes, withhold all food for 12 to 24 hours, but let the dog have a little water or some ice chips. If there is no sign of fever and the vomiting subsides, you can give the dog several small servings of easily digestible foods, such as kibble with a little scrambled eggs or rice, over the next 24 hours. If the vomiting does not recur, the normal diet can be resumed the following day. If vomiting continues or intensifies, or if you should notice any blood or worms in the vomit, consult a veterinarian immediately.

Some Siberian Huskies tend to gulp their food. Because of a quick intake of air into the stomach, the dog may suddenly regurgitate the meal. For dogs prone to this behavior, the best solution is to serve several small meals each day rather than one or two large ones, thereby limiting the amount of food in the stomach at any one time.

Constipation

Constipation is more common in older dogs or in those that chew meat bones. It usually occurs after a dog undergoes a sudden change of diet. Confining a dog for too long a time may also cause this problem as the dog restrains its natural urges to eliminate until allowed outside. In such cases, the problem usually is temporary and can be alleviated by administering a mild laxative, such as Milk of Magnesia (ask your veterinarian for the proper dosage, based on your dog's weight).

If your dog is prone to constipation, add a little extra roughage or one tablespoon of mineral oil twice daily to its normal diet to aid proper elimination. If the condition lingers, your veterinarian may suggest using a glycerine suppository or a warm water enema to alleviate the blockage.

If you ever see the dog actively straining, crying out with pain, and not passing any excrement, seek professional care at once. The dog may have swallowed an object that is now lodged in the intestinal tract, causing a life-threatening situation. Alternatively, a tumor or other growth may be present in the intestines. These situations require specialized veterinary care.

Impacted Anal Glands

At the base of the dog's anus are two sacs that secrete a strong-smelling substance used by the dog as a scent marker. The anal sacs, sometimes referred to as the "stink glands," normally are emptied during defecation. If, however, they are not cleared completely by the normal elimination process they can become impacted and will require manual emptying. Have your veterinarian show you this procedure the first time, as proper technique is required so as not to hurt the dog.

The symptoms of impacted anal sacs include a constant licking of the area and/or dragging the anus across the ground or floor (this if often referred to as "scooting"). Check the dog carefully, as a dog may also scoot simply because there is feces collected in the anal hair.

If the anal sacs appear full, they can be expressed manually by carefully pressing along the outsides and back of the sacs with your thumb and forefinger positioned on either side of the gland. Be sure to hold a tissue below the

gland to collect the fluid that flows out. If this procedure seems painful to the dog or if there is any pus or blood mixed in with the fluid, an infection may be present that will require veterinary attention.

Breed Anomalies

Hip Dysplasia

Hip dysplasia (HD) is a congenital malformation of the hip joint that causes an improper fit of the hip socket and the femur bone. Improper nutrition or overfeeding during the first year or two of life can increase the incidence of HD. In active dogs, such as the Siberian Husky, constant friction in an afflicted hip slowly wears the joint down, ultimately leading to pain when walking or during sudden movement. Although steps can be taken to relieve the pain and slow the course of the disease, there is no cure. Severely dysplastic dogs can be helped by hip surgery or hip replacement, but this is a painful and expensive solution. The first clinical signs of the disease generally do not appear until the dog is two to three years old, unless the animal is severely afflicted.

Because HD is hereditary, the best way to eliminate the problem is by breeding only those dogs that are not predisposed for the disease. Unfortunately, some Siberian Husky lines have a tendency toward HD. It is estimated that 5 to 10 percent of today's Huskies have HD. To protect the breed from this disease, breeders should have all dogs intended for breeding x-rayed when growth has stopped (at approximately 24 months of age). The X rays are then sent for evaluation by specialists from the Orthopedic Foundation for Animals (OFA) or by at least two board-

This veterinarian is examining a five-week-old male Husky puppy.

certified veterinary radiologists at a university veterinary school. The OFA will issue a certificate, rating the condition of the hips. Only those dogs certified as clear of the problem should be used in any breeding program. The X rays should be repeated yearly, if the dog is to continue in a breeding program. Unfortunately, although no guarantee exists that a dog will not develop HD, the chances can be minimized. Dogs that appear free of the disease can still pass along the trait if they carry a recessive gene for the trait.

Elbow Dysplasia

Like hip dysplasia, elbow dysplasia is a hereditary disease that afflicts a small percentage of Siberian Huskies. It is a malformation of the joints in the elbow. As with HD, the OFA can evaluate and certify elbow conformation on a pass or fail basis after reviewing X rays.

Eye Disorders

Siberian Huskies have a slight tendency to some eye disorders. Approximately 6 to 8 percent develop bilateral cataracts and 2 to 3 percent are afflicted with progressive retinal atrophy. These conditions are found in both sexes, regardless of eye color. If left unchecked, the dog will suffer a loss of acuity and eventual blindness. Ask your breeder if there have been any cases of this associated with his or her stock (a reputable breeder will tell you if this has happened and what was done to eliminate the problem from their breeding stock).

Remind your veterinarian to check your Husky's eyes carefully at the annual exam.

If there is any hint of a problem, the dog should be taken to a veterinary ophthalmologist. To make owners aware of this problem, many local breed clubs sponsor clinics to help diagnose these conditions.

Emergency Procedures

In emergency situations, speed is most important. If your dog sustains a serious injury, your first act must be to calm and restrain the dog so that it cannot move about and cause further damage to itself before you can transport it to a veterinarian. Internal problems may be present that are not visible to the eye.

You must also protect yourself from being bitten. Because the dog is terrified and may instinctively lash out at anyone who comes near it, be sure to approach the animal cautiously. Speak to it in low, soothing tones. A stocking, a tie, or a thin piece of cloth will serve as an emergency muzzle. (You should never use a muzzle on a dog that has chest injuries or is having difficulty breathing, however.) Fold the material in half and place a knot at the midpoint. Make a second loop approximately 6 inches (15.2 cm) above the knot, and place the dog's muzzle in the hole formed between the two. Pull the top loop tight over the muzzle, with the knot remaining above the jaw. Take the two ends and cross them under the jaw and around to the back of the head. Tie a secure knot, but be sure it is not too restrictive. You are now ready to assess the dog's physical condition.

Do not move an injured animal unless absolutely necessary (such as to remove it from a site where it may incur further damage). Inspect the skin and locate the source of any bleeding. If possible, gently wash the area with soap and warm water. If the blood flow continues, apply a clean cloth or gauze pad to the site, secure it if possible, and hold the compress in place until the bleeding subsides. Unless the cut is very small, it will need professional attention. A veterinarian will be better able to apply a bandage that will stay in place.

If it appears that a bone has been broken, immobilize the dog to the best of your ability. If allowed to move about, the dog may do damage to the muscles, cartilage, and nerves surrounding the break. Try to keep the dog calm, and get it to emergency treatment as quickly as possible. If necessary, you can use a blanket as a makeshift stretcher for transporting the dog short distances.

If the dog lapses into unconsciousness, check that its breathing passages are open. Get the dog onto its side. Gently pry open its mouth, and pull the tongue forward to allow airflow into the lungs.

In all of these situations, shock can quickly set in. Cover the dog with a blanket for added warmth, and monitor its heart rate. Never give an injured dog anything to eat or drink, especially alcohol. Knowing the dog's vital signs may help the veterinarian.

Poisonings

Even though it may seem that your Husky will eat just about anything, poisonings are not all that common, especially if all poisons are kept locked up. Most accidental poisonings occur without the owner ever knowing that the dog has ingested a poisonous substance. This often has serious consequences as *immediate* action is required if the dog is to survive a serious poisoning. Symptoms of poisoning include diarrhea, vomiting, lethargy, spasms, shaking, dizziness, and a color change or bleeding of the mucous membranes.

If you know the cause of the poisoning and have the packaging, you may be able to look for information regarding the proper antidote. Your local poison control center also may be of help. It will help your veterinarian greatly to know how much poison was ingested and when so as to formulate the proper method for removing it from the dog's system. Various procedures are used, depending on what type of poison has been ingested. Sometimes the stomach is pumped; sometimes the poison is neutralized in the stomach.

Household items are the most common sources of poisoning, not only for house pets but also for children. Keep all cleaning agents, pesticides, and painting supplies locked up. Antifreeze particularly is dangerous, as it is highly poisonous but has a pleasant odor and taste that attract the dog. Many house and garden plants are poisonous if chewed or eaten. Included among these are philodendron, poinsettia, and daffodil bulbs.

Caring for Elderly Siberians

With good basic care throughout its life, your Husky should remain vigorous and healthy for many years. As it ages, its digestive system probably will be the first to give it problems. Although constipation is common (often because of prostate problems), changes in the dog's diet can help alleviate this. Elderly dogs should receive a premium diet specifically formulated for the digestive systems of older dogs. These foods generally contain easily digested meats and a lower level of protein. Your veterinarian may also suggest that you add several teaspoons of bran to the dog's daily meal and may prescribe vitamin supplements, especially if the dog appears run-down. An adequate supply of water should always be available.

Elderly dogs tend slowly to lose weight, which is the first sign of a degeneration of the ability of the liver and kidneys to properly manage waste materials. If you notice a weight loss, be sure to have the dog checked by your veterinarian to rule out any life-threatening condition. Adding a little extra fat to the diet often will help many elderly dogs retain their weight.

Allowing tartar to accumulate on a dog's teeth throughout life often results in dental problems in elderly dogs. The elderly dog may have sensitive teeth, and this inevitably will cause it to stop the heavy chewing that removes tartar. Bad breath is common. Although a weekly brushing of the teeth can minimize this, plaque removal by your veterinarian often is required.

Even if your Siberian Husky has been spared the problem of HD throughout its life, it may develop a general joint stiffness as it ages. Arthritis is common for many dogs and can be aggravated in a dog that has been quite active throughout its life or in one that has become overweight. If your dog is bothered by this condition, avoid letting it climb stairs whenever possible and do not play games that require sudden turns or jumps.

TRAINING YOUR SIBERIAN HUSKY

Leadership Position

Regardless of breed or sex, dogs—as pack animals—exhibit a consistent pattern of behavior that affects the training process, and every Siberian Husky owner who wants a well-mannered dog must recognize this. Husky or Chihuahua, it's really all the same: A dog will assume that it is the boss until proven otherwise. I call this the leader-of-the-pack syndrome.

At birth, the dam assumes the leadership position in her pack and keeps her young in line. As the puppies begin to assert their independence, she will remind them of their place through low growls, a swat of the paw, or an occasional shake of the neck. Little else is necessary. She admonishes her young swiftly, fairly, consistently, and unemotionally, and they respect her position as leader. The wise owner follows the dam's example.

Consistency and Respect

If the dog misbehaves, respond accordingly and appropriately. Consistency is vital. Letting a dog's "cute little antics" go uncorrected will undermine an owner's leadership position and encourage the dog to misbehave again.

Once your Husky has mastered the basics, you can proceed to advanced training such as dog sledding.

Respond firmly but fairly every time the dog acts up, letting it know what behavior is expected and what will not be tolerated. Brute force is not required and is extremely counter-productive. The Siberian is a spirited breed and undoubtedly will test its owner's authority occasionally, but its gregarious nature can be shattered if it is treated brutally. When a dog is testing your authority, correct in a manner the dog will understand—a firm vocal reprimand, a stern look, a quick shake of the neck with your hand (being careful to just surprise the dog, not injure it). Correct it as its mother would, as the dog already should understand the method and the meaning. Little more should be necessary to make your displeasure clear if you are carrying out the corrections authoritatively. Be sure never to whine, nag, plead, or preach at the dog, as these clearly are not the actions of a leader, and the dog will not feel compelled to obey.

Although this may sound more like psychology than discipline or training, please keep in mind that obedience is based on respect. The dog must respect you, or it will not obey (unless out of fear, which is totally destructive to the owner/dog bond). The lessons that follow are general outlines regarding how to teach and discipline your dog in a way that will yield a well-mannered companion.

Rules to Train By

It is useless and frustrating to begin training a puppy before it is capable of understanding what you want. However, lessons in good house manners can begin when the dog first enters the home. The dog's first successes can be learning and responding to its name, coming when called, catching on to what *"No!"* means, and starting to learn the *sit*. Concentration is the key. If the puppy constantly wanders off, either physically or mentally, it is probably too young for formal training.

The lessons should be short at first, about ten minutes, but held *regularly*, two or three times each day. Repeat all lessons frequently, but not to a point where the dog can no longer concentrate or show interest. Boredom can do serious damage to a training program, and Huskies can be bored easily.

The atmosphere should be serious, but not unpleasant. Encourage the dog to perform well for you. Praise each minor success, but don't go overboard and make the dog so excited that it forgets the purpose of your time together.

All commands should be given with a firm, authoritative tone of voice. The tone is very important. Be careful not to sound as if you continually are scolding the dog or, even worse, pleading. Be sure to issue the same command each time you request a certain action (not *"Reba, come"* one time and *"Come here, girl"* the next). The simpler the better. As a general rule, you should include the dog's name in any command requiring motion *(come, heel)* but omit it from the commands that require the dog to remain motionless *(sit, stay, down).*

To be effective, each mistake must be corrected immediately with a verbal, *"No!"* Repeat the command, show the dog the proper response, and praise it when successful. Try to keep your talking to a minimum. Use simple, clear commands, and repeat the command only when necessary. Your goal is to have the dog respond correctly after only one command. A dog that needs constant prompting is not responding correctly.

Progress slowly, as an action quickly learned often is forgotten quickly. Build each day on the success of the previous lesson. Patience and consistency are the keys to success. Many repetitions are necessary before the dog can be expected to truly understand how it is to respond to any given command.

Regardless of how smart or willing the dog, mistakes will be made throughout the learning process. Correct fairly and with love, not out of anger. The dog most likely is making mistakes out of confusion, not willful misbehavior. Never shout at or strike the dog, as this will only worsen matters. Emphasize the dog's successes rather than its mistakes.

By keeping the lessons short and pleasant, the dog will remain eager to learn. Do not be tempted to push the dog beyond its capabilities, even if things are going well, as this can lead to exhaustion and disinterest.

End each lesson with a lot of verbal praise and petting, and turn to a pleasant activity, such as a walk, a run, or a game. Giving the dog a little special attention after a job well done lets the dog know you are pleased with its performance. With such positive reinforcement the dog will learn to regard training as pleasurable, not as a drudgery.

Training Puppies

Although Siberian Huskies can be quite adept at learning, they can also be bored and distracted easily. All training must enforce the idea that learning can be fun and will bring positive responses from the owner, but it must be clear from the start that training is not a game. It need not be unpleasant, however. Early successes—and a little creativity by the owner—are the keys to piquing and sustaining interest in training.

Although it may sound elementary, getting the dog to respond to its name is an important lesson. This task is accomplished easily by using the dog's name whenever you want it to come and by praising the dog lavishly when it responds. The dog will react happily to the attention it is getting and will subconsciously note how you react when you are pleased. This is the puppy's first success. It discovers that a correct response brings rewards. Huskies thrive on such positive reinforcement. The dog bonds to you and learns to want to please you. The dog's desire to please its owner is the backbone of a training program and must always be fostered.

The Primary Tools

Collars

Although you may want to familiarize the young puppy with the feel of a collar by having it wear a lightweight one when young, no collar really is necessary until formal training is to begin. At this time, you will need a training or choke collar, which consists of metal links with a ring on each end. This collar should be worn only during teaching sessions. It allows you to apply as much pressure as necessary to evoke the correct response or action by the dog. When pulled upward, the collar will tighten momentarily around the dog's neck. Once the pressure

is released, it will loosen immediately. The dog will learn quickly that the upward tug indicates displeasure and that a correction is needed. The choke collar is a valuable teaching aid that should never be used to hurt the dog.

Choose a collar that is the correct size for the dog—not one it will grow into. The collar should measure approximately 1 to 2 inches (2.5–5 cm) more than the diameter of the dog's head. A choke collar is designed to provide quick, snap-tight corrections. It is pointless to buy oversized collars because they will not close quickly and can, in fact, be dangerous if allowed to hang down loosely.

To form the collar, slip the chain through one of the rings. The lead can then be attached to the free ring. The side of the chain connecting to the free ring must be placed over the top of the neck, not under. In this position, the collar instantly will release whenever the upward pressure is removed. Although few Huskies complain when given a collar, you might want to let the dog wear it for a day to get accustomed to the added weight around its neck.

Lightweight Collars. If you want your dog to wear identification, select a lightweight collar that can be left on the dog at all times. Attach a small metal medallion listing the dog and owner's names, address, phone number, and any health problems the dog may have.

Training Leads

The training lead is made generally of nylon, woven cloth, or leather. Most people use a 6-foot (1.8-m) lead, $\frac{1}{2}$ to 1 inch (1.3–2.5 cm) in width, although a 3-foot (1.2-m) lead sometimes is used when more control is necessary. If the dog tries to chew the lead, correct with a firm *"No!"* and give the lead a light upward tug

to remove it from the dog's grasp. Many puppies will feel awkward and frightened by the tug of this sudden weight around their necks, so you may want to let the puppy drag the lead behind it for a short time. Monitor the situation closely in case the dog becomes frightened and to make sure it does not get tangled and possibly hurt.

Once your Husky has adapted to the feel of the lead, pick up the lead but apply no overt pressure on the dog's collar. Walk around with the puppy for several minutes, following wherever it wanders. Now let the pup know it is time to follow you. If all is progressing well, introduce the feel of the upward tug whenever the puppy moves out and tries to pull on the lead. The puppy usually will be stunned by this intrusion—sometimes annoyed. Reassure it that there is

Your reaction is a puppy's first cue to its success—use a lot of praise when training.

nothing to be afraid of, but continue to apply firm pressure whenever it wanders out of your control area. Using quick corrections, you should be able to make it clear to the puppy that the lead is a restraint and that the tugs require corrective action on its part. Once this is clear, formal obedience lessons can begin.

The Basic Commands

Regardless of how you intend to use your Siberian Husky, it must learn five basic commands: *sit, stay, heel, come,* and *down.* Until a dog willingly performs these commands, it should be considered untrustworthy and should be kept on a lead or removed from activities where self-control is required. This is not punishment; it is restraint. Participation should be the dog's reward for learning proper behavior and self-restraint.

Owners are responsible for teaching their Husky the basic commands. Siberian Huskies are, by nature, quite intelligent and can be capable learners if the owner knows how to keep the dog's attention and interest. Your task is to teach your dog to obey you instantly, with only one command. Accept no less, as the Husky most likely will try to get away with a

Once your dog is used to its leash, formal training can begin.

less-than-perfect performance if you let it, as there is a definite stubborn streak in the breed.

Huskies are not known for their concentration powers, so make the task as easy as possible for everyone involved by practicing the early lessons indoors in an area free from distractions. The dog should be on a lead for all of the basic exercises.

Sit

When performing properly, the dog will sit at your left side, with its shoulders square to your knee. Position the dog at your side, with the lead in your right hand. Keep the lead taut, applying a slight amount of upward pressure to help keep the dog's head up. Command the

dog "*Sit*" while you press your left hand on its rear and place it in the sitting position. If the dog moves out of position, use your left hand to straighten it while your right hand continues the moderate upward pressure from the lead. Praise the dog when it is properly positioned, and release with "*Good dog!*" and/or an upward sweep of your left hand.

It is important to praise the dog when it reaches the *sit* position, not when it gets up. It must learn to associate the praise with the sitting action.

The first *sits* should be quite short, so that the dog has little chance to tire of the position and slump over on your leg or lie down. You want to emphasize success. Gradually increase the *sit* time. If the dog moves out of position, correct with "*No!*" and a light jerk from the lead, then put it back in place.

Once the sitting action becomes habitual in response to the command, there should be no need for you to touch or press on the dog's rear. At this point you can begin training the *stay* and *heel* commands.

Stay

You should not begin teaching the *stay* until the dog reliably is performing the *sit*. The *stay* command builds from the *sit*. Place the dog in a *sit*, keeping some upward pressure on its neck from the lead in your right hand. As you command "*Stay!*" you simultaneously take one step away from the dog, beginning your movement with your right leg (which is the farthest from the dog). Bring the palm of your left hand down toward its face, stopping just short of its muzzle. The hand signal must be made at the same time that the command is given and the step is taken. Retain eye contact, if possible. Repeat the

command while maintaining the signal in a voice that is firm and authoritative.

Do not expect the dog to stay for more than ten seconds or so at first, so release after a small success and praise.

When the dog breaks the *stay*, return it immediately to the *sit* and repeat the whole procedure. Your Husky undoubtedly will try to move toward you once it sees you move away, or it will try to lie down. Be patient and do not expect immediate results. Correct each infraction and try again, but do not bore the dog with endless repetitions. Move on to another exercise, and spring the *stay* on the dog every now and then—not continuously. Praise each minor success lavishly.

Slowly extend the length of the *stay* and the distance you move away from the dog each time. A well-trained dog can be relied on to stay in the *sit* position for several minutes.

Placing the dog in a *sit-stay* is an excellent way to deal with the breed's natural desire to jump up and greet visitors. Whenever a visitor comes to the door, make the dog sit throughout the initial greeting. If possible, have one person stay with the dog while another answers the door. Have the newcomer ignore the dog at first, as this will lower the dog's interest in jumping. As the Husky matures and masters the proper greeting, you will hopefully not have to resort to an extended *stay* whenever someone comes to your door.

Heel

An untrained Husky surely will surge ahead of its owner when on a lead, pulling the hapless owner along for a ride. This bad habit should not be tolerated and must be stopped while the dog is still young. Heeling is no more than a controlled walk, and every Husky should be required to perform it.

Always place the dog on your left side, its chest preferably in line with knee. Hold the lead in your right hand and use your left to supply corrective jerks.

The *heel* starts with the dog in a *sit.* Move out with your left foot first, commanding *"Reba, Heel!"* as you move forward. Snap the leash as you give the command to start her forward, removing the pressure as she responds. Walk at a comfortable pace, and jerk the lead only if she surges ahead or lags behind. Make your snaps quick and firm, and repeat *"Heel!"* with each correction. Praise the dog as soon as she responds, using a pleasant tone and *"Good girl!"* Repeat the praise as you are moving if the dog remains in proper position, but don't overdo it and interfere with the dog's concentration.

When you stop, the dog is to sit at your side. In the beginning you will need to issue the *sit* command; however, as the dog becomes adept at heeling the *sit* should become automatic when you stop and no verbal command should be needed.

Learning the *heel* will take time, and your Husky may lose its concentration quite frequently. As you encounter problems—usually surging ahead—you may have to stop and place the dog in a *sit* to restore calm. This certainly is preferable to continually snapping the dog back into position, and it allows the dog to succeed at a task it already is familiar with, and thereby receive praise. This will keep everyone at ease and help the heeling practice continue rather than break down into confusion n the dog's part and anger on the owner's. Once the dog successfully has completed the *sit,* move out again with *"Reba, heel!"* Praise

if she comes and moves in the proper position. Stop as soon as she misbehaves, giving a firm tug on the lead and a stern look.

If the dog continues to surge, you must continue to break this pattern by stopping. Do not apply continuous pressure from the lead on the neck of a surging dog, as this will mean that the choke continually is applied. The choke should be used sparingly to regain the dog's attention and bring about a correction. It is to be used only when needed and should be released immediately. Many Huskies are impervious to the shock of the snap of the standard choke chain. I've had good results by adding a startling sound in addition to the corrective neck jerk, which is accomplished by just slapping my own thigh to make a popping sound. If this doesn't work with your dog, you may need to consult a professional trainer in your area about selecting a more effective training collar for your dog.

Keep the early heeling attempts short—no more than 10 to 15 minutes. When the dog becomes more adept and no longer needs to be put into frequent corrective *sits,* you can extend the lessons as energy and interest permit. Once you get the dog to heel properly and not surge, the walk will become a great time to share each other's company.

Come

The *come* is quite easy to teach, as Siberian Huskies instinctively will respond to the sound of their master's voice and will seek out the sound. The *come* teaches a dog that it must return to its master at once, without hesitation.

In most situations, even puppies happily come when called, in anticipation of play, food, or various pleasant exchanges. The biggest obstacle to overcome is what I call the "What's in it for me?" syndrome. The goal of the *come* command is to structure this response so that the dog will obey your call regardless of the circumstances.

Begin training the *come* command with a pleasant play period. Place the dog on a long lead or rope (20 feet [6.1 m] or more works best) and let it play in the practice yard. Hold the lead but maintain only minimal tension. Once the dog is relaxed and occupied with some nearby object, command *"Reba, come!"* in a firm tone, and snap the lead to start the dog moving toward you. Praise as the dog *begins* to move. Have her come directly to you and into a *sit.* Should she fail to respond, give a sharp correction with the lead and repeat *"Reba, come!"* If necessary, repeat the command and reel the dog in by slowly retracting the cord (but this rarely is required).

Once the dog has completed the *come* and gotten into a proper *sit,* release with *"Good girl!"* and let her roam once more. Repeat the command at various intervals, and enforce with a sharp tug on the lead should the dog ever fail to move toward you immediately.

The *come* should be used and practiced only sparingly. Although you should test the dog on it no more than once or twice in a training session, you can use it at various points throughout the day when the dog's presence really is requested. Praise highly when the dog responds and do not allow the dog to ever ignore the command.

If you need to correct your dog for an offense of any kind, *go to it* and reprimand. *Never command the dog to come and then punish it when it arrives.* If you call the dog with *"Come!"* and then proceed to punish it when it arrives, you almost certainly will ruin your chances of having a dog that instantly will return to you when called, thus negating this command's importance and reliability.

Down

The *down* command builds from the *sit* and *stay* commands. To teach your Husky to lie down, begin by placing it in a *sit* while you kneel by its side. As you command *"Down!"* grab its front legs near the body, gently lift them from the floor, and lower the dog to the ground. Once down, command the dog to *"Down, stay!"* Praise with *"Good dog"* if it remains in the prone position. Your left hand can rest on the dog's back to deter it from getting up, if necessary. Release from the *down* by motioning upward with your hand and gently tugging the lead. The dog should then return to the *sit* position.

***Before long this five-week-old puppy can begin training to learn the proper* sit.**

With practice, your dog can eventually maintain a down-stay for extended periods where it can relax across the room from you.

With this command, the downward movement needs to be reinforced, and the concept must clearly be differentiated from the *stay*. Do not make your dog remain in the *down* position too long at first, but be sure it remains lying on all fours. The dog is to be alert on the *down*, not overly sprawled out.

The *down* can be practiced several times each day. As the downward movement becomes more familiar, you no longer will need to lower the dog's legs. During this transition, try issuing the command and just slapping the floor with the palm of your hand to get the dog moving down. You also can try placing the lead under your left foot, keeping it rather taut, and as you command *"Down!"* add a slight pressure on the dog's shoulders to get it moving down.

As the dog progresses, teach it to lie down on the lead from various positions, such as in front of you or from a distance. It is very useful to incorporate a down motion with your hand at the time of the *down* command to augment these exercises. When working indoors, practice the *down* off leash. Never accept a sloppy performance once the lead is removed. This may sound a bit harsh, but a Husky should never be allowed off leash in an unconfined outdoor area. An exciting scent or

CHECKLIST

Problem Solving

When problems are encountered, ask yourself these questions to help you evaluate what works best (or doesn't work at all) with your Siberian.

✔ Are your commands clear, concise, and consistent?

✔ Are you giving the dog ample time to learn, not rushing it?

✔ Do you speak in a firm, authoritative tone (never shouting, scolding, or whining)?

✔ Do you praise the dog enough to make learning a pleasant experience?

✔ Are *you* concentrating?

If you feel the problem is with the student and not the teacher, observe the dog's behavior and body language.

✔ **Is the dog easily distracted?** This is very typical of Huskies. You may be training in an area that presents too many distractions for a beginner. Try a more secluded training site and see if the dog's concentration improves.

✔ **Is this lapse a new or constant occurrence?** A sudden disinterest or confusion in a male can be caused by a local bitch in heat. Alternatively, the dog may have reached a temporary learning plateau (common during the fifth or sixth week of training) and may appear to have forgotten all it has learned. This odd phenomenon is not unusual and generally passes in a week.

✔ **Is the dog ill?** Many illnesses are hard to spot. A dog that is reluctant to move freely or jump may be showing the early signs of HD. Eliminate the health issue with a thorough examination by a veterinarian.

the sight of something moving in the distance may lure away even a well-trained and disciplined Husky—and it can be nearly out of sight in just a moment's time. It is good discipline to train the dog to perform an extended *down-stay* daily. With practice (and some Huskies need *lots* of practice at this), you will be able to have your dog remain in a *down-stay* for 30 minutes or more. This will reinforce your position as leader in the dog's mind and will give you the control you need at times to remove the dog from any undesirable activities (such as hanging around the dinner table or getting underfoot when company comes)—and you won't have to lock it up. A properly trained dog can be placed in an extended *down-stay* near its owner, yet in a place where it can relax too, such as across the room or in a corner.

Begin with *stays* of a few minutes and gradually increase the time, but do it irregularly (10 minutes, then 8 minutes the next time, 15 the next). With this approach, the dog cannot anticipate when it will be finished, and it truly will learn to obey the command.

Huskies invariably will become bored and try to break the *stay*. Tell it *"No, stay!"* and replace it. As the dog becomes accustomed to the long *down*, it often will fall asleep. This is perfectly acceptable as long as it remains where it was placed when it awakens. You should make it a point to wake the dog with a tap of the foot near its head when it is time for the release. Do not let it sleep on indefinitely, as you need to formally complete the exercise for it to have any impact. Always end the long *down-stay* with the upward release motion and then give the dog great praise, as this exercise requires a lot of self-control, which is not a cornerstone of the Husky temperament.

The "emergency" *down* also can be an effective lifesaving command to immediately stop a dog from participating in or entering into a dangerous situation. Once you are certain that the dog understands the *down* concept, the *down* can be practiced while walking, not just from the *sit*. Teaching a dog to drop on command while in motion takes time, but is well worth the effort. If your Husky somehow find a way out of your yard and wanders near traffic, you could use the *down* to drop the dog immediately to the ground until you could retrieve it. Few Huskies have any car sense, and this command could save a dog's life. Such a case illustrates why only an *immediate* response to the command can be acceptable.

Training Problems

There are as many training methods as there are trainers, so rest assured that there is no foolproof method for training all dogs. Do not get discouraged if your dog is not learning as quickly and efficiently as you had expected. Various problems often arise that interfere with the learning process. Your dog may just not be able to adapt to the training method you have selected. Finding the solution to a training problem generally is a matter of trial and error and, most of all, patience and perseverance. The most obvious place to start is to evaluate your teaching technique.

If, despite your best efforts, disorder still prevails in your training program, consult a professional trainer (preferably one experienced with Siberian Huskies). An expert eye often can spot quickly if there is an underlying problem and propose corrective measures. Many times all that is needed is a new approach or technique that the dog will understand or like better. Sometimes the owner needs a lesson in how to better discipline the dog or keep its interest.

Never let training setbacks—and there will be some—escalate to the point where you lash out at the dog or give up in despair. Help from a more experienced trainer usually is a good investment in your dog's future.

Advanced Training

Owners of Siberian Huskies will find that the breed can excel in many sports and types of competition.

Show-quality Huskies are among the most popular entries at AKC conformation shows (such as all-breed shows—like Westminster—or specialty shows, where only Siberians are judged). In this type of competition, the entrants are judged on their physical appearance against the guidelines of the breed standard.

For training enthusiasts, Siberians can learn the skills required for Obedience competition. Obedience trials are held under AKC auspices, with competition at novice, open, and utility levels. There are training clubs dedicated strictly to this sport, and Obedience trials routinely are held in conjunction with most large AKC conformation shows. There are also some less common sports that are tailor-made for Siberian Huskies.

Dog Sledding

A sport in keeping with this breed's heritage is the sled dog degree program. The goal is to demonstrate the ability of the Siberian Husky in sled dog racing competition. The program is open to all purebred Siberian Huskies individually registered with the AKC. Competition is in

three degree levels, based on experience and distance. There are three types of races: sprint, distance, and triathlon.

Pack Dog Programs

The newest performance program sponsored by the Siberian Husky Club of America (SHCA) is the working pack dog program, which recognizes the achievements of Siberian Huskies participating in verifiable hiking trips as an active member of the hiking party, such as cross country excursions, hiking trails, or back country hikes. Dogs in this program may compete for two titles. The dog must carry a canine pack with an initial weight equal to 25 percent of the dog's body weight. The pack may be lightened during the course of travel because of the consumption of food, water, and other supplies, but the ending load cannot be less than 10 percent of the body weight.

Above: Patience is crucial when training; don't get discouraged if problems arise. Below: A display of the Huskies' dog sledding abilities in competition.

Agility

Agility is a fast-paced sport in which the dog must navigate over various types of jumps, tunnels, and other obstacles. The dog and

A Siberian Husky at the Westminster dog show.

handler are working against the clock and other exhibitors. Agility originated in England and was brought to this country by the United States Dog Agility Association (USDAA). The AKC began sponsoring Agility trials in 1994. Many owners of Siberian Huskies find Agility a wonderful pastime with their pet.

Therapy Work

One of the most fulfilling activities a Husky can engage in is therapy work. Research has proved that animals enrich the lives of humans in ways that can reduce stress and make them happier and healthier. Organizations throughout the world, such as Therapy Dogs International or the Delta Society, currently are engaged in developing programs in which well-trained dogs visit elderly, sick, or emotionally disturbed people, as well as prisoners. The dogs are therapeutic aids that can help people in many ways—as aids for those struggling to recover from debilitating illnesses, such as a stroke, or as loving enticements for withdrawn and uncommunicative children. This pet-facilitated therapy has proved highly successful, and the cost is usually just a matter of a few hours time.

Housebreaking should not be a battle; it should be accomplished quickly if handled properly. The owner must be vigilant if housebreaking is to be learned quickly. The first thing to know is *when* the puppy will need to eliminate: after waking, after eating, after strenuous play, first thing in the morning, and last thing at night. There also will be in-between times, and the puppy usually will give some physical cues: it looks uneasy, sniffs the ground, and walks in circles, as if searching for something. Quick housebreaking depends in large part on the attentiveness of the owner: knowing when the puppy will need to eliminate, monitoring its physical signs, getting it to the proper elimination area in time, and praising every success.

When paper training your dog, always place it on the paper when you think it needs to relieve itself. When your dog does so, praise it highly.

Housebreaking should be dealt with rationally and with common sense. Regardless of the eagerness of the dog, until four to six months of age, a puppy has limited bladder control. Until a puppy truly understands what is expected, mistakes are inevitable. The owner must react in a firm and fair manner the puppy will understand. Do not overreact when you find an unwanted deposit. To make a connection in the dog's mind with your displeasure and the waste, bring the dog to the spot. Point at the excrement and have it look. Scold in a low, guttural tone. Immediately bring the dog to the proper elimination area. Praise the dog if it should go there. When you both return to the house, banish the dog to its sleeping quarters for a short "time out" and then clean up the mess out of the dog's sight. Never hit the dog or rub its nose in excrement.

To avoid having a stain that reattracts the dog to the spot, be sure to wash each accident site with a solution designed to specifically remove urine odors (available from veterinarians or at pet stores) or with a soapy solution containing a little vinegar. Do not use an ammonia-based cleaner, as this may reattract the dog to the spot.

Aiding the Task

Puppies must be monitored when let out for elimination. During the training period, make the extra effort and go out with the puppy. It needs instruction on where to go and, most of all, praise when it succeeds.

Restrict where the puppy may go until it is reliably housebroken. When not under direct supervision, the dog should be confined to two areas: the sleeping quarters and the elimination area. The sleeping quarters should be a small, uncarpeted, puppy-proof area with all escape routes blocked off. A mesh baby gate will do well while the Husky is quite small. The elimination area should be outside, rather than a papered area in the house. The intermediate paper step is necessary only if the owner cannot be present in the home for long periods during the training process. Bring the puppy to the elimination area each time it shows signs of needing to go, and praise each success.

Crates

A crate is the most efficient method of housebreaking. As pack animals, dogs instinctively seek out the confinement and security of a den.

Well-constructed dog crates are made of heavy-duty plastic

or wire mesh and can be purchased from pet shops and dog supply stores. The crate must be large enough for the dog to comfortably sit or lie down in, but not so large as to give the dog plenty of room to subdivide its confines into a bed area and an elimination area.

A crate can be a valuable housebreaking tool when used in conjunction with a regular schedule of walks and feedings. The owner must take the dog to its proper elimination area at regular intervals and enthusiastically praise the dog each time it relieves itself there.

Although the owner may remain in the room with the puppy during the first few cratings to help it feel at ease, occupy yourself with an activity and pay no outward attention to the puppy unless there are signs of distress. Huskies are very intuitive, and if they sense anxiety or guilt in their owner's behavior, they may use this to their advantage. Alternatively, they may decide that the crate really is something to be afraid of because their owner is obviously upset by it.

At first, crate the puppy for only five to ten minutes. This time can be increased gradually over the next few weeks. During the day, puppies under 12 weeks of age may remain in the crate for up to one hour; puppies 12 to 16 weeks of age may be crated for up to two hours; older puppies may stay a maximum of three to four hours in a crate. The time a dog spends in its crate should be based on the dog's age and elimination requirements and will vary from dog to dog. All ages can be crated overnight.

The crate should be situated out of the direct line of household traffic, but not somewhere that will make the dog feel isolated. Line the bottom of the crate with a blanket for added comfort and give the dog a chew toy or bone to help relieve any boredom. Bowls of food or water do not belong in the crate during the housebreaking process.

The crate is a very valuable housebreaking aid.

Paper Training

Although paper training is the slowest method of housebreaking, it is an effective—even vital—method for those who cannot be with their puppy for long stretches of time during the day.

The unhousebroken puppy should be confined to a limited space whenever it is not being supervised directly. Divide the space into three separate areas: elimination area, feeding area, and sleeping or crate area. Line the elimination area with several layers of newspapers.

Place the dog on the papers every time you think it needs to eliminate. Encourage the puppy with *"Do your business"* or any similar phrase that does not include the terms *"Come," "Sit,"* or *"Down,"* which will be used later as basic obedience commands. Placing a small piece of previously soiled paper on each new pile will help reattract the dog to the elimination site. Praise the dog enthusiastically whenever it uses the papers. It quickly should learn that this spot is acceptable for elimination. Shrink the size of the newspaper pile until it is quite small, and place it outside a few times if necessary to let the dog know that the new elimination spot is acceptable.

BREEDING QUALITY SIBERIAN HUSKIES

From the earliest days of the Chukchi dogs, breeders have worked hard to preserve the traits, instincts, and abilities that make the Siberian Husky special. Siberian breeders are among the most adamant of the purebred fanciers, willing to forgo widespread popularity for the breed in their zeal to keep it from falling prey to the haphazard breeding methods that often take over when supply cannot satisfy demand.

To preserve breed integrity, matings should be carefully planned events. A breeder's goal should be to produce puppies that are of equal, or hopefully *better,* conformation quality than the preceding generation. Random matings usually do little to retain the positive breed traits and strengths of the parents; rather, such matings add the possibility of new faults being produced in the offspring. The breeder's task is to select the best possible breeding partners in the hopes of producing the best possible offspring.

The sections that follow outline some guidelines for formulating a breeding program.

Selecting a Sire and Dam

When planning a mating, the breeder's most important job is to find a top-quality sire and dam that will complement each other. The

Breeding quality Siberian puppies is a serious matter.

potential sire and dam should be evaluated for their strengths and faults, as compared with the breed standard. A dog's outward appearance is a result of the set of genes it received from its parents. That outward appearance is no guarantee of the dog's ability to pass on these traits to its offspring. It may have hidden traits that are not expressed physically, but that still can be passed on.

Selecting which dogs are suitable for breeding should be based on a history of quality genes that have been passed through the generations. Experienced breeders can determine this by reviewing pedigrees for qualities that consistently have been expressed in succeeding litters of puppies. Novice breeders often mistakenly assume that by breeding champion with champion you will produce future champions. This may or may not work. Although sire and dam may each be of superior conformation, each may carry genes for traits that do not complement the partner's. Puppies are often of lesser conformation quality than the parents.

Most experienced breeders base their kennels around the brood bitch. It may be quite difficult to secure a top-quality bitch from a breeder, who naturally will be reluctant to part with a promising female puppy. When starting out, many breeders begin with a proven quality-producing adult bitch from an established kennel (again, if the breeder will part with her). This eliminates the uncertainty of breeding a maiden bitch, but such proven producers usually are quite expensive.

When selecting a stud, the emphasis should be on finding one that complements and enhances the qualities of the bitch. An experienced stud that already has produced quality offspring is, of course, preferable. A good Siberian Husky stud should be of correct size and be well balanced, be a good mover, and have a good coat, proper bite, and sound temperament. He should be as free as possible of obvious faults.

Beginners should consult an experienced breeder whenever possible. Such a breeder can help evaluate the faults and strengths of the potential sire and dam, and later evaluate the quality of the litter produced. This information can be vital to the success of a kennel.

When planning a mating, study the pedigrees of the potential dam and sire to see if the two dogs share any common relatives. Hopefully, a pedigree was supplied when you purchased your dog. If not, ask the breeder to reconstruct this information, if possible. A pedigree is a very useful tool for determining from which type of breeding system your dog stems.

Breeding Systems

The three basic types of breeding systems are *linebreeding, inbreeding,* and *outcrossing.* Although all of these systems aim to strengthen desirable traits and eliminate faults through selective breeding, they go about it in different ways.

Linebreeding

Linebreeding is the mating of related dogs that are removed from each other by at least one generation (for example, cousin to cousin,

grandson to grandmother). The sire and dam typically share a common quality ancestor in the second or third generation that is known to pass on its desirable traits to its progeny. Linebreeding enables a breeder to "fix" correct type in her or his stock by breeding quality genes in successive generations. This limits the flow of new genes into the breeding stock.

Inbreeding

Inbreeding is the mating of closely related dogs, such as sister to brother, daughter to father, or mother to son. These matings intensify the genes present in the bloodline, as no new genes are introduced.

This system, when used by knowledgeable breeders, can fix type quickly and bring uniformity to desired traits in a line. It also can enhance any faults. Faults that normally would lie dormant because they are recessive traits are more likely to be expressed in inbred animals because of the limited number of possible gene combinations. These faults ultimately can be eliminated, however, as those animals exhibiting or carrying the trait would be removed from the breeding program. Inbreeding can be an effective method when used sparingly by knowledgeable, experienced breeders. It rarely is used in successive matings and usually is combined with linebreeding techniques.

Outcrossing

With outcrossing, a breeder attempts to eliminate faults by pairing dogs that hopefully will complement each other. The dogs to be mated do not share common ancestors in the first five generations, but each is selected because it has shown itself able to pass on the quality traits the other lacks. This is not random selection. For example, a stud from a line known for good hindquarters would be chosen for a bitch from a line possessing good fronts but weak hindquarters. Hopefully the resulting offspring would retain her good fronts and his good hindquarters.

Outcrossing usually is used when linebreeding fails to correct a particular fault, and a line that is thought to be complementary is used to compensate. Outcrossing adds new genes to the bloodline, rather than intensifying ones that already are present.

Unstructured outcrossing is the usual pattern for neighborhood litters (Mr. Smith has a Siberian dog; Mr. Coyle has a Siberian bitch). There is no known common link. For the purposes of this discussion, this type of mating would not be considered a true breeding system.

Preparing for Breeding

A bitch must be physically and mentally able to withstand the rigors of whelping and raising a litter of puppies before being bred. Most bitches do not reach this state of maturity until at *least* their second heat. A healthy bitch can thereafter be bred every other season until approximately six or seven years of age if all previous whelpings have been uncomplicated. Siberian Huskies usually are fairly easy whelpers.

A stud dog can produce offspring when less than a year old and can continue into his teens. It is advisable, however, to use a Siberian stud dog that is between the ages of one and eight. At approximately eight years of age, the stud's fertility begins to decline.

The beginning of a bitch's heat cycle or "season" is marked by a noticeable swelling of the vulva, which becomes hard to the touch. This is followed shortly by a watery discharge that may later become tinged with blood. A bitch will be ready for mating on approximately the tenth day after the onset of her cycle. In the early days of the cycle, she is attractive to males but will not allow coitus. Ovulation generally occurs around the ninth day into the cycle, after which time she is fertile.

Mating

Planned breedings often involve dogs from different kennels. The female usually is brought to the stud dog for most stud services, as females generally will adapt quickly to a new environment and are not as easily unnerved by strange surroundings as males.

The bitch and stud dog must both be in good physical condition at the time of the mating. A bitch being considered for breeding should be examined by her veterinarian approximately 30 days before her expected heat cycle to evaluate her health and to determine if any inoculations or controls for internal or external parasites are needed. Both dogs should also be tested for canine brucellosis, a highly infectious disease that results in fertility problems.

At least two handlers should be present at the mating to soothe and control the animals, if necessary. The bitch often is muzzled. The stud will mount the female from the rear, his front legs resting around her middle. Once penetration and ejaculation have occurred, a section of the stud's penis will swell and the two dogs will be "tied" together for up to 30 minutes. The handlers should remain and supervise until the tie is broken naturally. Any attempt to force a break of the tie can have

serious consequences for both the stud and bitch, so both dogs must be kept calm during this time. To ensure a successful fertilization, the bitch generally is bred twice, with a day's interval between matings.

Pregnancy

Approximately 63 days is the normal gestation period for puppies. A bitch in whelp may have a slight increase in appetite and some minor swelling of the breasts, but generally there is little physical evidence of pregnancy during the first few weeks. A veterinarian should be able to confirm a pregnancy at approximately four weeks after mating, but the owner should never try to feel for puppies dur-

This female Husky pup is sleeping by her littermate with eyes wide open.

ing this time, as this can cause serious damage to the dam and puppies.

The bitch should eat the same well-balanced diet that she is used to throughout the pregnancy. No supplementation usually is needed in the first four or five weeks. She will require additional calories (primarily in the form of protein) during the last weeks, with a 30 to 50 percent increase in food being needed by whelping time. To minimize discomfort, reduce the size of her meals and feed her more often (three or four times a day).

A bitch in whelp should be encouraged to perform her normal daily routine and to exercise. She will need good muscle tone for an easy delivery. Do not allow any vigorous exercise during the last two weeks, or any jumping, pulling, and much climbing of stairs.

A whelping box will be needed for the bitch to deliver the litter in and to raise the puppies for several weeks. This can be purchased from pet stores and supply outlets or can be constructed at home. The box must be low enough to allow the dam to come and go, yet high enough to keep the puppies confined while small. It should be large enough to allow the bitch to lie on her side and stretch out, but not so large that puppies can crawl

Siberian Husky litters usually contain six to eight puppies.

too far from the warmth of their mother. It is advisable to build a guard rail several inches in width, placed several inches up the sides, to serve as a barrier preventing the mother from crushing the newborns against the sides of the box. The bottom should be lined with layers of newspaper, which can be removed easily. The whelping box must be placed in a warm, dry, draft-free location that is not a high-traffic area.

The bitch will slow down her activities and seek out her "nest" when delivery nears. Be sure she is familiar with the whelping box before delivery is imminent and that she has time to become comfortable with it. If not, she may devise her own spot to have the puppies.

The following supplies will be needed for the delivery: washcloths, a heating pad, blunt-tipped scissors, waxed dental floss, a scale, paper towels, a wastebasket, and a lined box or bed to place newborns in while others are being born.

Delivery

Approximately 24 hours before delivery, a bitch's temperature will drop to around 99°F (37.2°C). As delivery becomes imminent, she is likely to become agitated and will begin to pant heavily. She may vomit when the abdomen begins contractions. She may be very anxious at this point, so speak to her constantly in soft, soothing tones. You should notify your veterinarian as whelping time nears. Inexperienced breeders should also ask a more knowledgeable breeder to assist them.

The puppy will arrive in a membrane sac, which must be removed to allow the newborn to begin breathing on its own. Should the bitch fail to tear the sac open and cut the umbilical cord, be prepared to perform this task. If you do not have an experienced breeder to help, get a thorough briefing from your veterinarian regarding the entire delivery process prior to whelping time. The placenta (afterbirth) normally will be expelled within several minutes of each birth. Keep track of the delivery of each placenta, as none should be retained. Do not be alarmed or surprised if the bitch eats a few of the placentas. This is quite normal and will not harm her.

Siberian Husky litters usually contain six to eight puppies. Allow the dam to lick and suckle each newborn, but remove the already born when the birth of the next whelp is in progress. At this time, you can gently wipe the puppy clean, weigh it, and temporarily place it in the heated holding box until all deliveries are over.

A good Husky brood bitch will have a gentle touch with her puppies, and a tolerance for onlookers. Praise her and offer a warm drink of broth once the final puppy has been expelled. A first-time mother should be monitored closely over the next few days to be sure she shows a healthy interest in her litter. If she should become agitated or aggressive with the puppies, seek immediate veterinary assistance for her and guidance on how to take over the care of the puppies.

False Pregnancy

Female Siberian Huskies that have not had at least one litter are prone to false pregnancies. The symptoms are practically identical to an actual pregnancy. About eight weeks after a heat cycle, the bitch will become restless. If there are no puppies for her to take care of, she will gather up and adopt substitute babies—balls, toys, bones, and so on. Although there is no medicine to prevent or alleviate this condition, she should be given plenty of extra attention, exercise, and love. Supplementing the diet can also help to minimize this condition. Bitches prone to this condition usually are spayed to prevent recurrence.

Caring for Newborn Puppies

The new litter will spend its first four weeks or so in the whelping box with its mother. During the first few days of life, the puppies will receive antibodies from the dam's colostrum (the first milk) that should protect them for the next six to ten weeks from most of the common contagious diseases. The puppies' first battery of shots will then take over.

It is essential to provide the litter with a warm environment—approximately 85 to 95°F (29.4–35.05°C)—for the first few weeks of life. Puppies cannot shiver properly at birth to keep themselves warm, so their body temperature rises and falls in accordance with that of the immediate surroundings. Their heat regulation is quite poor until about four weeks of age, and during cold weather they must get supplemental heat. This can be done by adjusting the entire room's temperature or by keeping the room at from 70 to 75°F (21.1–23.9°C) and adding additional heat (covered water bottles, heating pads, infrared bulb lamps) to the whelping box. With this method, you must be very careful and monitor the box constantly, as the puppies can be burned easily or become overheated.

Husky dams normally are very dedicated mothers and will attend to all the basic needs of their puppies. They will not only feed them but also will stimulate them to urinate and defecate and clean up their wastes by ingesting them.

The owner's prime responsibility during the first few days is to carefully attend to the dam's needs and keep the whelping box very clean. Check to see that each puppy is nursing and that none is away from the warmth of the mother. Each newborn also should be picked up and checked regularly for overall health, and its weight gain should be recorded. Consult with your veterinarian if any puppy does not seem to thrive by the third day.

The owner may need to carefully trim the puppies' nails with baby scissors at approximately two to three weeks of age. Puppies tend to knead with their paws against their mother as they nurse, and sharp nails can scratch and be quite painful for the dam.

Siberian Husky puppies quickly turn into adorable fluff balls, and it is easy to shower them with lots of love. Newborns can be stroked gently, caressed, and softly spoken to from birth. This will begin the human/dog bonding process.

The puppies' eyes will begin to open at 10 to 14 days, but it will take another week before they can focus properly. The ear canals begin to function at about 12 to 17 days. Stimulation, such as soft music and visual backgrounds, encourages prompt development of the senses.

Weaning the puppies onto solid food can begin at approximately three weeks of age. This begins the puppy's transition to adulthood, and breeders should give their dogs a lot of attention during this time. By handling each puppy as much as possible, talking softly to it, and giving it a daily grooming with a soft brush, the owner will help accustom the puppy to what life is going to be like with humans. Having the wriggling puppy hold still for a brushing is also its first introduction to humans as "alpha" figures.

Siberian puppies show from the start the cheerful exuberance that is so characteristic of the breed. They grow quickly but lose little of the zest for life that is so bountiful in the newborn pup. It can be said that the Siberian remains a pup at heart throughout its life.

Organizations

American Boarding Kennel Association
4575 Galley Road
Suite 400A
Colorado Springs, CO 80915

American Society for the Prevention of
 Cruelty to Animals (ASPCA)
441 East 92nd Street
New York, NY 10028

American Veterinary Medical Association
930 North Meacham Road
Schaumberg, IL 60173

Canine Eye Registration Foundation
South Campus Court, Building C
Purdue University
West Lafayette, IN 47907

The Delta Society
P.O. Box 1080
Renton, WA 98057

Humane Society of the United States
2100 L Street N.W.
Washington, DC 20037

Orthopedic Foundation for Animals
2300 Nifong Boulevard
Columbia, MO 65201

The Seeing Eye
P.O. Box 375
Morristown, NJ 07963

Therapy Dogs International
P.O. Box 2796
Cheyenne, WY 82203

International Kennel Clubs

The American Kennel Club (AKC)
260 Madison Avenue
New York, NY 10016

United Kennel Club
100 East Kilgore Road
Kalamazoo, MI 49001-5598

The Kennel Club
1-4 Clargis Street Picadilly
London W7Y 8AB
England

Canadian Kennel Club
2150 Bloor Street West
Toronto, Ontario M6S 4VT
Canada

Australian National Kennel Council
Royal Show Grounds
Ascot Vale
Victoria
Australia

*This boy and his Siberian pup are beginning
the human/dog socialization process.*

Sled dogs must learn to work together as a team.

Irish Kennel Club
41 Harcourt Street
Dublin 2
Ireland

New Zealand Kennel Club
P.O. Box 523
Wellington, 1
New Zealand

The current Corresponding Secretary for the Siberian Husky Club of America, Inc. is:
Fain Zimmerman
210 Madera Drive
Victoria, TX 77905-0611
Since new officers are elected periodically, contact the AKC for the latest information.

Books

Alderton, David. *The Dog Care Manual.* Hauppauge, NY: Barron's Educational Series, Inc., 1986.

American Kennel Club. *The Complete Dog Book.* New York: Macmillan, 1992.

Baer, Ted. *Communicating with Your Dog.* Hauppauge, NY: Barron's Educational Series, Inc., 1999.

Battaglis, Carmelo. *Dog Genetics: How to Breed Better Dogs.* Neptune, NJ: TFH Publications, 1978.

Benjamin, Carol Lea. *Mother Knows Best: The Natural Way to Train Your Dog.* New York: Howell Book House, 1985.

Klever, Ulrich. *The Complete Book of Dog Care.* Hauppauge, NY: Barron's Educational Series, Inc., 1989.

Lorenz, Konrad Z. *Man Meets Dog.* London and New York: Penguin Books, 1967.

Rice, Dan. *The Dog Handbook.* Hauppauge, NY: Barron's Educational Series, Inc., 1999.

About the Author

Kerry Kern, formerly Managing Editor of the *Canine Graphic*, has written extensively on the subject of dogs. She is the author of *Rottweilers*, *Labrador Retrievers*, and *The New Terrier Handbook*.

Photo Credits

Tara Darling: pages 2–3, 4, 8, 16, 20, 21, 28, 36, 52, 53, 68, 73, 80 (bottom), 81, 93; Paws for Pictures: pages 25, 37 (top), 48, 84, 89; Connie Summers: pages 12, 13, 32, 33, 37 (bottom), 40, 44, 45, 48, 56, 60, 65, 72, 76, 77, 80 (top), 84, 88, 89, 92

Cover Photos

Norvia Behling: front, inside front, back, inside back

© Copyright 2000, 1990 by Barron's Educational Series, Inc.

All inquiries should be addressed to:
Barron's Educational Series, Inc.
250 Wireless Boulevard
Hauppauge, NY 11788
http://www.barronseduc.com

International Standard Book No. 0-7641-1041-1

Library of Congress Catalog Card No. 99-55897

Library of Congress Cataloging-in-Publication Data
Kern, Kerry V.
   Siberian huskies : everything about purchase, care, nutrition, breeding, behavior, and training / Kerry V. Kern ; drawings by Michele Earle-Bridges.
    p. cm.
   Includes bibliographical references (p.).
   ISBN 0-7641-1041-1 (pbk.)
   1. Siberian husky. I. Title.
SF429.S65 K47   2000
636.73—dc21   99-55897
                          CIP

Printed in Hong Kong

9 8 7 6 5 4 3 2

Important Note

This book discusses buying, keeping, and raising Siberian Huskies. The publisher and the author think it is important to point out that the advice and information regarding Siberian maintenance applies to healthy, normally developed animals. Anyone who buys an adult Siberian or one from an animal shelter must consider that the animal may have behavioral problems and may, for example, bite without any visible provocation. Such anxiety-biters are dangerous for the owner and for the general public.

Caution is further advised in the association of children with a Siberian, in meetings with other dogs, and in exercising the dog without a leash.